Praise for *Zen Wrapped in Karma Dipped in Chocolate*
and Brad Warner's *Hardcore Zen*

"What's dipped in Brad's Zen chocolate treat? Generous helpings of wisdom and ample swirls of common sense, all sprinkled with humor!"                 — David Robbins, Hollywood composer

"By turns wickedly funny, profane, challenging, and iconoclastic ... Warner constantly focuses on the importance of a direct experience of reality in all its rawness over adherence to any set of beliefs — even Zen ones.... Entertaining, bold, and refreshingly direct."
                                        — *Publishers Weekly*

"Warner brings the same tough, skeptical attitude to Zen that he brought to punk rock.... Profane and sometimes irreverent; capable of devastating, corrosive humor; offering nothing gentle or conventionally reassuring, Warner pulls no punches."         — *Booklist*

"It's rare to encounter someone who can claim authority on such a wide variety of the useless and profound, but Warner has the résumé to back it up. Warner isn't looking for converts. Rather, he sees Buddhism as a truth-seeking method, a means of confronting reality."                                    — *CityBeat*

"Brad's story illustrates how it's possible, even natural, for the ideals of punk and Zen philosophy to peacefully coexist."
                                        — Bookgeek.com

# ZEN WRAPPED IN KARMA
# DIPPED IN CHOCOLATE

# ZEN WRAPPED IN KARMA DIPPED IN CHOCOLATE

## A TRIP THROUGH DEATH, SEX, DIVORCE, AND SPIRITUAL CELEBRITY IN SEARCH OF THE TRUE DHARMA

## BRAD WARNER

NEW WORLD LIBRARY
NOVATO, CALIFORNIA

New World Library
14 Pamaron Way
Novato, California 94949

Text design by Tona Pearce Myers

Library of Congress Cataloging-in-Publication Data
Warner, Brad.
Zen wrapped in karma dipped in chocolate : a trip through death, sex, divorce, and spiritual celebrity in search of the true dharma / Brad Warner.
    p.   cm.
ISBN 978-1-57731-654-1 (pbk. : alk. paper)
1. Religious life—Zen Buddhism. 2. Warner, Brad. 3. Spiritual biography—United States. I. Title.
BQ9286.2.W37 2009
294.3'4442—dc22                                                  2008044941

First printing, February 2009
ISBN: 978-1-57731-654-1

Printed in Canada on acid-free, 100% postconsumer-waste recycled paper

Ｇ New World Library is a proud member of the Green Press Initiative.

10  9  8  7  6  5  4  3  2  1

# CONTENTS

# INTRODUCTION

*I*n 2007 my mom died and then my grandmother died, my wife decided she didn't want to be my wife anymore, I lost my dream job, and people I thought were my friends and colleagues in Buddhist practice began attacking me in public over scandals that existed solely in their own minds. Only one thing was clear by the end of the year. I was going to have to start all over again.

I'm a Zen Buddhist teacher, a "Zen master" to use a common, but very much mistaken, term.* Buddhism is intended to help people deal with suffering. A Zen master, at least in the popular conception, is a mystical being, an Enlightened One who can rise above all human affliction and discontent. This year life opened a whole big can of suffering on me. How does a real Zen master — as opposed to the cartoonlike figure invented by pop culture — deal with death,

---

* I honestly don't know where the term *Zen master* comes from. It sounds like something from a bad *Charlie Chan* movie, circa 1936, to me. I use it ironically to call attention to the fact that even a dork like me has attained the rank so often translated as Zen master, or "the Venerable," or "His Holiness," or whatever. The irony is often lost on some readers. But not on you, I'm sure.

divorce, job loss, and personal discord? How does he* perform the work of trying to help others get over their tough times while going through some pretty heavy shit of his own? How do you sit and meditate while your world crumbles all around you? Is meditation a valid reaction or just a form of spiritual escapism? These are all reasonable questions. They're questions I asked myself a lot that year.

This is my third book. You don't need to read the other two to understand this one. But in some sense this is episode three of a series, and we need a little "previously in Brad's books" thing to bring everyone up to speed. My first book, *Hardcore Zen: Punk Rock, Monster Movies, and the Truth about Reality*, was an autobiographical account of how I made the transition from hardcore punk rock bassist to Zen Buddhist monk. I also tried to lay out some of the fundamentals of Zen Buddhist philosophy. Zen is essentially a "back to basics" form of Buddhism that emerged in China maybe a thousand years or so after Buddha died (he died around 480 BCE). Over those thousand years, Buddhism, which had begun as a very simple practice and philosophy focused on seated meditation, had acquired a whole lot of other stuff — gods, demons, chants, statues, big-ass temples filled with elaborate paintings, and all kinds of other similarly useless junk. The Zen movement sought to strip all that away and get back to what mattered, the bare-bones meditation practice Buddha had discovered as he sat under a ficus tree looking for the truth. There's more to it than that, of course. But that's it in a nutshell.

I discovered Zen entirely by accident when I was the eighteen-year-old bass player for the Akron, Ohio–based hardcore punk band Zero Defex (aka oDFx). At the time, the early 1980s, hardcore punk was the loudest and toughest kind of music there was. It was also a social movement intended to create a more realistic framework in which to understand the world. In Zen I discovered something far more powerful and real than hardcore. Yet I never stopped being a

---

* Or she, but I'm sure you know Zen teachers can be either gender.

punk rocker. In fact, Zero Defex re-formed about a year after the book came out, and we still play shows when we can get together.

My second book, *Sit Down and Shut Up: Punk Rock Commentaries on Buddha, God, Truth, Sex, Death, and Dogen's Treasury of the True Dharma Eye*, got deeper into the specific Buddhist philosophy that I practice and teach. That philosophy stems mainly from the works of Dogen Zenji, a thirteenth-century Japanese Buddhist monk who wrote lots of deeply philosophical tomes, as well as a ton of extremely nuts-and-bolts manuals on how to practice and live the Zen way. Sometimes he mixed the two so thoroughly it'd make you dizzy. In one chapter he's telling you about the nature of being and time, and in the next he's writing about how a monk should take a dump. No joke, folks. He really *does* devote an entire chapter to how to use the toilet. Dogen did not consider this to be the least bit ironic. To him, taking a dump and examining the nature of being and time were exactly the same thing.

I lived in Japan when I wrote the first book. But while I was writing the second I moved to Los Angeles and began, for the first time, trying to teach Buddhism in the country of my birth. Because of the two books I found myself becoming the very thing I had always hated — a religious authority figure, a spiritual celebrity, a famous Zen master. People began to expect me — of all people — to be the thing they envisioned a Buddhist master ought to be. But let me clue you in on a little secret, friends and neighbors. Not only am I not that thing, but no one is. No one. Not even what's-his-face whose smiling mug graces the cover of every other issue of the big Buddhist rags by the checkout counter in your local new age bookshop.

I began to see that it was necessary to demonstrate that in a very clear and unambiguous way. Some folks have tried this before. But they usually try by pointing outward, away from themselves. There must be a hundred tell-all accounts of some spiritual teacher's transgressions — their big cars, their drug habits, their bizarre sexual peccadilloes.

The underlying assumption often seems to be that although that guy wasn't the real deal, maybe somewhere out there *someone* is.

*Shoes Outside the Door* by Michael Downing presented the story of the scandalous downfall of Richard Baker Roshi,* the dharma heir of Shunryu Suzuki Roshi, author of *Zen Mind, Beginner's Mind.* Baker Roshi was perceived by some as the spiritual superman they sought until his abuse of power, money, fame, and sex became too flagrant to attribute to some kind of "crazy wisdom" spirituality. In her book *The Great Failure*, Natalie Goldberg revealed the truth that rather than being the "clean" — a word she repeats so many times it gets annoying — Enlightened Master they all thought he was, Dainin Katagiri Roshi actually had — *gasp!* — sex with a few of his students.** It was time someone told the story of what it's like to do this very unusual job from inside. I'm not the first to do it. But the practice is still far too uncommon.

When Zen Buddhism and other forms of so-called Eastern wisdom first became trendy in the West in the sixties and seventies, many followers tended to see their teachers as supernatural creatures. Unlike Western religions, many Eastern spiritual traditions had this idea of the "enlightened being," of which the teacher was supposed to be an example. This idea seemed to suggest that the teacher was a kind of Christ-like paranormal creature with powers and abilities far beyond those of ordinary people. Plenty of folks still make a bundle by playing the role of the spiritual superman. It's a scam. It's important to show that all of us in this Eastern spiritual master game are no more supernatural than any Catholic priest, rabbi, minister, shoe salesman, or fishmonger.

A lot of people out there have a vested interest in not having

---

* *Roshi* is an honorific term for a Zen teacher that comes after the person's name. Some people mistake it for a last name. It's not.

** And, by the way, Goldberg herself never did it with Katagiri. None of the women Katagiri actually slept with felt the matter was worth writing a book about.

anyone say the kinds of things I'm going to say in this book. Their livelihood depends on their followers believing that they're something they are not. Maybe this book will make it a little more difficult for some of those people to get rich that way. I certainly hope so. I guess that sounds mean. But the people who do that sort of thing are doing untold damage not only to their followers but to themselves as well. They would be better off if they had to get jobs at the local In-N-Out Burger instead.

To do the damage that needs to be done to the absurd idea of the Eastern spiritual master as superhuman, I'm focusing on the events in my own life in 2007 as specific examples of how Zen teaching and Zen practice are very much human activities performed by real people in the midst of real-life problems. Zen does not offer the kind of neat and pretty "ultimate solutions" promised by so many religions and cults. Instead, it is unrelentingly realistic. Yet it does provide an exceptionally practical way to deal with what life dishes out to all of us. In fact, I believe Zen practice and philosophy provide the only truly rational and realistic way to live a balanced and happy life. Some people don't like it when I say that. They'd rather I told them that Zen was just one of many good ways to deal with stuff. But if I thought that way I wouldn't be teaching and writing about Zen, and I probably wouldn't even bother practicing it. This doesn't mean I want everyone to convert to my way of thinking or that I want to destroy all other religions and philosophies. It only means that I'm not interested in teaching or even practicing anything other than the philosophy I believe to be the best in the world.

I had another question when I came back to America after eleven years: does real Buddhism exist in the West? After I returned I began to be invited to speak and practice at a lot of Buddhist centers around the country. I had the opportunity to see firsthand what went on in the name of Buddhism both in the places I visited and through the people who visited and contacted me and showed me the results of their practice. While I've found shining examples of the Buddha's way in prisons and at heavy metal shows, I've also seen sad perversions of Buddhism in its very own temples and among those supposedly propagating the Way in America. Authentic Buddhism doesn't always come packaged the way we imagine it should.

There is something very profound, perhaps we can even say holy, in every human being. We all have access to this something every moment of every day, but most of us will live our entire lives without even suspecting it exists. The Buddha was not full of shit when he said the cause of suffering could be uprooted and that you can put an end to it once and for all. There is a way out of this mess humanity has found itself in. It's just that the answer to the cause of suffering — and the way to end it — are nothing at all like what you think they are or imagine they should be.

# CHAPTER 1

# ZEN DEATH TRIP

**M**y mother's piercing howl careened off the walls of the museum, like the noise a coyote might make if you tied it up in the middle of a granite cave and started sawing off its tail. The high, hard walls amplified her screech, ricocheting it from one room to another so it could be heard by everyone inside — the schoolkids on their field trips, the grandmas and grandpas out for a pleasant afternoon, the art students dressed in black trying to pick up other art students dressed in black. Everyone turned to see who was torturing the poor old woman in the wheelchair.

My dad and I tried our best to keep her quiet. It was hard to know for sure what she was trying to communicate. She used to be an art student herself and always liked museums. But her speech, once full of deep insights and bad jokes, had degenerated into a single, all-purpose yowl. Happy, sad, urgent, bored: it all came out exactly the same. She didn't really seem upset. But she wanted to say something, and none of us had any idea what it was. We finally tried wheeling her up to a painting. She quieted down and studied the colors and brushstrokes. She used to be a painter herself, though her real forte was charcoal drawing. For a moment she was almost like she used to be twenty years before. Then she started howling again.

The Zen Death Trip* with my mom and dad to see my grandma took place in the late summer of 2006, a few months before my mom died. Although my mom wouldn't actually die until January 2007, Dad and I both pretty much knew this was probably the last journey she'd be taking. Neither of us would say so, though.

Here's why we knew. My mom and dad were both sixty-five by then. My mom had been diagnosed with Huntington's disease about

---

\* I didn't make up the phrase Zen Death Trip, by the way. When I was a student at Kent State University in the early 1980s I lived in a place they called the f-Models house because a local punk band called the f-Models lived there and rehearsed in the basement.

Iggy Morningstar, the band's leader, shared a room upstairs with his girlfriend, Lisa, but she kicked him out for being drunk all the time and never paying rent. Then Iggy hanged himself. Iggy's death was the end of punk rock for me for a very long time.

Up till then I'd been deeply committed to punk. Reagan and Brezhnev were determined to burn the planet to a cinder before I could graduate from college. Yet the entire nation seemed to be in deep denial. It was my sacred duty to scream that message as loudly and as often as possible.

By the time Iggy died, though, our little punk scene in Akron had already been infiltrated by brain-dead jock dudes who saw slam dancing as a way to get wasted and beat up on anyone smaller than themselves. I didn't want to play background music for assholes fighting anymore. Iggy's death just sealed the deal. His band was the first punk rock band I had ever seen in real life and was a tremendous influence not just on me, but on the whole scene. If Iggy wasn't gonna fight the fight anymore, why should I?

Iggy and Lisa's room was taken over by another KSU student whose name I can't remember. I'll just call him Larry, though. He looked like a Larry. He was tall and wiry, and he was really into riding bicycles. He was also into the Nichiren Shoshu sect of Buddhism. They said the best way to attain salvation was to chant "Nam Yoho Renge Kyo" — which means roughly "the Lotus Sutra is the coolest sutra of all" — over and over while kneeling in front of a little miniature Lotus Sutra. So Larry used to do that a lot up in his room.

One day I noticed that Larry was wearing a little pin that said Zen Death Trip on it. He told me it was something one of his bicycle-riding buddies had made after a particularly grueling ride he and Larry had taken. Because of Larry's affiliation with Buddhism, they'd named it the Zen Death Trip, even though Larry wasn't actually a student of Zen per se.

twenty years earlier. Huntington's, if you don't know — and most people don't, so don't feel bad — is a degenerative neuromuscular disease similar to Parkinson's. A person who has Huntington's gradually loses control of their muscular functions until they pretty much can't do anything for themselves. After a while they look something like Stephen Hawking, scrunched up in a wheelchair with their face all contorted and their limbs not doing anything they ask them to. Unlike Stephen Hawking, though, if you're a Huntington's patient, you usually end up losing your mind as well. Or that's what they say. Then you die.

The progress of my mom's illness had been pretty slow. So up until a few years ago you could mostly understand the things she said, and she could handle herself okay. She could walk if someone helped her keep her balance. She could go to the bathroom by herself if someone helped her in and out.

But all the things she had managed to keep together started falling apart one by one. Dad used to shield the family from a lot of this, pretending that Mom was doing for herself a lot of the things he'd actually started doing for her. By the time we took the trip she couldn't walk at all. Oh, she *insisted* that she could walk. But it was more like you'd drag her around. She said very little that you could understand. She couldn't go to the bathroom without a tremendous amount of help. And for the last two years or so she hadn't been able to feed herself. Mom really should have been in a nursing facility with a full-time staff. But unfortunately she was American, and my dad worked independently as a sales rep for various companies in the rubber chemical business. So there was no way he could afford professional help. Besides, he was deeply in denial about the whole thing. Interestingly enough, he was never in denial about being in denial. He openly admitted to it. But he refused to admit that he could no longer care for her by himself.

Mom's disease probably pushed me into studying Buddhism more than any other factor in my life. Two of my aunts, Mom's sisters, had started showing symptoms long before Mom did. My mom's own mother had died from the disease not long after I was born. I'd known since I was a child that we had a deadly disease in the family. By the time I was a teenager I was aware that, according to the experts, I had a 50 percent chance of inheriting it. When I was in junior high I was so massively uncoordinated and terrible at sports that my parents suspected I might have the juvenile form of the disease. The specialists they took me to discovered that the real problem was that I had one very bad eye and one very good eye. The resulting near total lack of depth perception made it nigh on impossible for me to judge whether I'd catch a ball or get hit in the nose by it. Since I hated getting hit in the nose by balls and then being made fun of for it, I hated sports. Since I had one very good eye I could still read and do all kinds of other stuff, so no one ever realized how bad my vision out of the other one was. Not even me.

My parents got me my first guitar as a way of seeing if I really was uncoordinated or just unmotivated. When I got a giant Fender Showman amp and started blasting the neighborhood with inept renditions of the Ramones' first album, Mom and Dad began to regret their decision. But it was too late.

Knowing early on that I could die a horrible death made me start looking for answers. I saw through the bullshit handed out by the churches I went to pretty fast. The burgeoning new-age movement, with its hippy-dippy fixation on spirit channeling and crystals, held my interest for about ten or fifteen minutes. Drugs promised enlightenment but only showed me what it was like to be unenlightened on drugs. The Hare Krishnas had nice songs and delicious food, but the more I looked into their philosophy the stupider it sounded.

I wasn't satisfied with fantasies about heaven or hell or dreams about reincarnating in a better place. I wanted to know about this life because I might not have it for very long. I wanted real answers, not bullshit. In my first year of college I was introduced to Zen Buddhism and the philosophy of Eihei Dogen by a teacher named Tim

McCarthy. What I found in Dogen's take on Zen was real. I tested it myself, and it worked.

When I say that Buddhism worked, I don't mean that it was a magic solution to my problems. Nor do I mean that any miracles happened or that I was able to erase all doubt and fear from my mind through some kind of special power. What I mean is that Buddhism, especially Dogen's Buddhism, provided the most truly realistic and practical way of dealing with life. It isn't spirituality, but it isn't materialism either. Dogen's Buddhism does what no other philosophy I've ever come across is able to do. It bridges the gap between these two forever mutually opposing ways of understanding reality. It negates both spirituality and materialism yet simultaneously embraces them. And it's more than just a way of thinking about things. There's a practice involved — zazen. You cannot separate the philosophy from the practice. If you don't do zazen practice you cannot ever hope even to come close to comprehending the philosophy.

My family is from Ohio. But Mom and Dad moved to a suburb of Dallas, Texas, in the early eighties when my dad left his longtime Akron-based employer, Firestone, to work for one of the new rubber industry companies down there. My sister, who was in high school at the time, went with them, but I stayed up in Ohio to finish college. So I never actually lived at the house my parents had in Flower Mound, Texas, for over two decades. By 2006 Dad had quit the company he'd been working for down there and was freelancing as a rubber chemical salesman.

About a month before we took our Zen Death Trip my eighty-six-year-old grandma, who lived near Cincinnati, where my dad grew up, broke her pelvis. My cousin Tina, who lived with her, has a son who is autistic. At age five, he could read and write and Google whatever struck his fancy, yet he couldn't talk intelligibly and he'd only just been potty trained. Apparently he was racing around Grandma's house one afternoon, as he often did, and smashed into Grandma, causing her to fall and break her pelvis. So now she was in some kind of a rehab place recuperating and learning how to walk again.

Coincidentally there was some kind of rubber chemical convention going on in Cincinnati where my dad could drum up some much-needed business. He decided it would be cool to take care of two things at once by visiting his mom and going to the convention. And since killing two birds with one stone sounded so attractive, he thought, why not try for three or four? So he decided to take Mom along with him so that she could visit with Grandma, since who knew how long either Mom or Grandma had left, *and* he decided to ask me to come along as well, since I could help look after Mom and I could see Grandma too, since I hadn't visited for a while.

As you may well imagine my mom didn't do airplanes too well by this time, especially in the post–9/11 era of massive airport paranoia. The last time Dad had tried flying with her somewhere, getting her wheelchair through security and then dealing with Mom's near constant howling on a crowded aircraft proved too much for both of them. So the only way this was gonna happen was if we drove from Dallas to Cincinnati. Now, ever since I was in high school, my dad's work has had him traveling long distances by car all the time. For him an eighteen-hour road trip sounds pretty easy. I'm not even sure if he can understand why other people think that eighteen hours in a car sounds kind of long.

And mind you, this isn't just any old eighteen-hour road trip. This is an eighteen-hour road trip with a woman who could barely walk, needed to have her undergarments changed every three hours, and liked to make a noise that sounded like someone had set fire to a live cow. I loved my mother dearly. But man, oh, man, that *sound.* . . .

Now, as if that wasn't enough, after my grandfather died six years before all this, my grandma discovered that he had left behind around half a million dollars. This was a major shock. Grandpa was not a rich man by any stretch of the imagination. He worked most of his life in a middle-management position at a paper factory and lived in a modest brick house he and his cousins had built by themselves back sometime before World War II. But evidently he'd made a few wise investments and had been socking away nearly every cent he earned into a couple of savings accounts. Over the course of his seventy-odd-year working life this had added up. He never told anyone about the money, not even my grandmother or my dad and his sister. And Grandpa didn't leave a will.

For the past six years that money had been a bone of contention between my dad and my grandmother. Dad thought she ought to be using that money to help him out with my mom. Besides being a nice thing to do, it would relieve her tax burden. And she wasn't doing anything with that money anyway.

So there was this big pile of money sitting in Grandma's bank account doing nothing but waiting for her to die so that everyone could go nuts over it. Word around the family had it that Dad was not in Grandma's will. Or maybe he was. Or maybe Grandma, like her late husband, hadn't written a will. No one would talk to each other straight about it. Grandma's version of the story changed every time she told it. It's possible that even she didn't really know. As upset as Dad was over having been disowned, my sister was even madder. She'd stopped talking to Grandma years ago.

And just FYI, I did not want the fucking money. They could keep it. I'll get my own money.* Free money is never free. Never, ever, ever. It doesn't work that way. You wish it did. I wish it did. But it doesn't.

In any case, Dad planned to have it out with his mother about this — for, like, the fifth time — when he got up to Ohio.

Given this set of circumstances, there was no way an eighteen-hour car ride from the Dallas suburbs to Cincinnati with my mom in tow to see Grandma was going to be anything other than a Zen Death Trip, even if no one actually got killed. And walking into it, I seriously wondered if any of us would survive.

---

* Please go out and buy six more copies of this book to give to friends. Thanks!

# CHAPTER 2

# LOS ANGELES

*B*efore I tell you all about the Zen Death Trip, though, I ought to tell you how I even got myself in the position to be taking it.

Fourteen years ago I moved halfway across the world, from Akron, Ohio, to Japan, because I figured it was a more reasonable alternative to killing myself. I was making records, but they weren't selling. I couldn't find a decent job. I felt useless and without direction or hope.

One day I threw a length of rope in my trunk and drove out to a park where I planned to hang myself from a tree so deep in the woods that nobody would ever find me. When I parked my car I saw some little kids playing on the swings. And I thought, there's nowhere I can do this where I can guarantee my body won't be found by those kids. Or by some young couple going for a stroll. Or by an old man out hiking. Or just someone who doesn't really want to see my dead body swinging from a tree. And just like I'd spent the past two decades bummed about Iggy's death, that person would be bummed about finding my stinking corpse. And my mom would be sad. My dad would be sad. My sister would be sad. All kinds of people would be sad. I couldn't do it. But I couldn't go on the way I had been either.

The Zen practice that I'd been doing since the early eighties was probably what saved me from taking the same way out that Iggy had. Before that I might never have considered the impact my death might have on others. I'd always had a romantic fascination with suicide that even Iggy's death hadn't cured. What finally cured it was when I had a clear enough head to look at the truth of the matter.

When my sister told me they were hiring teachers in Japan I knew I'd found a way to kill myself without actually killing myself, a way to leave absolutely everything behind, to disappear. So I went for it, and I got the job.

After I'd been in Japan just over a year, working as a teacher, I took a completely different job with a film- and TV-production company. I left them after a little while and then joined a similar company in the same industry — Nakano Productions. What I'm going to say about them is all true, but not necessarily strictly factual.

Nakano Productions was founded in 1961 by a Hajime Nakano, the special-effects man who created a very famous and extremely profitable Japanese movie monster that has been variously described by Western film critics as a "terrible pterodactyl with radioactive tonsillitis," a "giant chameleon with daggers for teeth," a "massive fanged and flying terrapin," and even a "ludicrous squid from space." Needless to say, these critics often failed to watch the movies they wrote about.

Nakano Productions struck it rich in the early seventies with a live-action (not animated) TV show called *Zone Robo*. *Zone Robo* concerned the exploits of a 120-foot-tall robot from outer space controlled by a little boy who routinely saved the world from gigantic monsters portrayed by men in ill-fitting rubber costumes stomping around in balsa-wood replicas of downtown Tokyo. *Zone Robo* was shown in the United States in the seventies, and I loved it. I was majorly psyched to be able to get a job working for the company that had created such an amazing TV series. It was a longtime dream of mine to make the show successful in America. Once I started working for the company, that became my mission.

But Nakano Productions is a strange company. Hajime Nakano was a creative genius, but not much of a businessman. When he retired in 1973 he left his company in the hands of his eldest son, Masaki Nakano. Masaki was not a terribly creative guy, but he was a terrific businessman. He turned his father's characters into big moneymakers in the eighties through shrewd deal-making and merchandising. It was Masaki who hired me as part of his dream to make Zone Robo "fly across America," as he liked to say. Unfortunately, about a year after I joined, Masaki left the company to join a bizarre religious cult. I used to see reports about the cult erecting satellite dishes in the mountains to try and contact the Bodhisattva Manjushri, or some such thing. No one ever spoke about Masaki after he left. In keeping with Masaki's wishes, the family and the company officially regarded him as dead. The company being worth millions and millions of yen, there thus began a battle for its control between siblings, cousins, uncles, and aunts, the likes of which Japan hadn't seen since the days of the warring samurai clans.

A whole series of interfamilial machinations that are far too complicated to lay out here soon ensued. After nearly a decade of infighting, things seemed finally to settle with two members of the Nakano clan, Tomoyuki and Ishiro, emerging from the bloody fray as president and vice president, respectively.

Tomoyuki and Ishiro hatched a plan to send me out to Hollywood to be Nakano Productions' liaison to the glittering world of the American film and TV industry. I feared that they'd send me out to the States with no real agenda and without the necessary decision-making authority to set my own agenda. But watching my mom's condition deteriorate with each visit home, I decided it might be better to be in America. Los Angeles was only two hours by plane to Dallas. I could visit every couple of months, or maybe even more often, to help out Dad and to just be there. So I accepted the posting.

For all the complaining about the company I will do in the following pages, I feel like I owe a lot to Nakano Productions. I love the company dearly. They were like my family when I lived in Japan. They also paid my Buddhist tuition. I used their liberal vacation policy to attend numerous Zen retreats. I used their computers to put the final touches on my first book. I even met my current teacher, Gudo Nishijima, while I was in Tokyo working for them. Nishijima Sensei* always kept a day job to support himself while he studied and taught Buddhism, and he encouraged his students to do the same. I figured if I could just set Nakano Productions up with a cool American movie deal, my job for them would be done. Whether or not I'd continue working with them after that, I hadn't really decided.

A lot of people see a huge conflict between being a Buddhist teacher on the one hand and working for a company that makes low-budget Japanese monster movies on the other. Sometimes I do too, to be honest. It certainly flies in the face of the usual image of the serene monk sitting in his mountain temple sipping tea and dispensing cosmic wisdom. But of course that image was always complete crap anyway.

There were times in the past when it was necessary for there to be full-time professional Buddhist monks.** Asian societies in the past understood this. They supported Buddhist monasteries and made offerings to wandering monks. Today this traditional support

---

\* The word *sensei* just means "teacher." Some Buddhist organizations in the States use the word as a term of rank. In their lineage a *roshi*, literally "old man," trumps a *sensei*. This usage of the two words is unknown in Japan and annoys the bejesus out of me when I come across it. I've always called Nishijima "sensei" because that feels most natural to me, even though he's been a roshi in the literal sense as long as I've known him.

\*\* By *monks*, I mean male and female monks. I don't think the word *nun* is very appropriate for what we have in Buddhism. Neither is *monk*. But that's another story.

system is fading fast, even in Asia. These days most Japanese Buddhist monks don't beg or even live on donations to their temples but support themselves by running funerals. Nishijima likes to say that the Japanese Soto school — in which he was ordained, by the way — is a guild of funeral directors.

Because we don't have any system in place to support them, most Western Buddhists, including most Western Buddhist teachers, need to have "real jobs" in the secular world. But there's a myth going around Buddhist circles in the West that the only jobs that qualify as what Buddha called "right livelihood" are as therapist or yoga teacher. This is bullshit.

There's an old parable about this. A Buddhist master walks by a butcher shop. In those days, butchers, whose line of work required them to violate the first and most important Buddhist precept, "Do not kill," were viewed as the ultimate symbol of wrong livelihood. The master watches a customer walk into the shop and ask, "Do you have any fresh meat?"

The butcher gently puts down his cleaver, folds his hands in a gesture of respect, and says, "Sir, do you see any meat in my shop that is not fresh?" From this interaction the master learned that even a butcher can do his job in a Buddhist way, with attention, care, and respect.

So my job just happens to be in monster movies. I like monster movies. It's a fun job, so I'll keep it as long as they'll have me, thank you very much.

Right livelihood is not restricted to a certain set of approved ways of making a living. It's a matter of what your intuition tells you about what you're doing. This can be a tricky thing, since most of us don't have a clue about how to listen to our intuition. It's not that absolutely anything you do for work is fine. Yet it's also not true that someone else can decide for you what's right to do. For some people, yoga teacher and therapist are absolutely the wrong occupations. What society — even a so-called Buddhist society — has decided about what constitutes a "proper job" is absolutely irrelevant.

Before I went to Japan, I worked at the Summit County Board of Mental Retardation and Developmental Disabilities helping mentally challenged adults work and live in this complicated world. I'm sure the "yoga teacher or therapist" crowd would applaud such work and be appalled that I left that job to work in the movie business. But I hated working at the Board of MRDD, and I did a piss-poor job. They're far better off without me. In the movie business I can provide a modicum of balance where it is sorely needed. What's better — a very conscientious butcher or a really lousy therapist? Which one has a greater potential to cause real harm?

After I arrived in Los Angeles I started checking out the city's Zen scene. Much of what I found was truly appalling. Zen Master Rama, whose real name was Frederick Lenz, had been one of the major players in the LA Buddhist scene. Fred was a skinny white man who liked to be photographed in a sexy leather jacket with a bright light behind his giant 'fro to make it look like he had a halo. He offered special classes "for the ladies" and taught high-priced seminars about what he called "Tantric Zen." Folks, there ain't no such thing as Tantric Zen. There is a Tibetan tradition called Tantric Buddhism, and there is a Japanese tradition called Zen. Calling yourself a teacher of Tantric Zen is like telling people you teach Jewish Catholicism. At these seminars folks could learn about higher planes of existence and energy flow manipulation or be regaled with tales of the master's work with Michael Jackson and other Hollywood luminaries. Master Rama committed suicide in 1998 by taking a bunch of pills and wandering into the ocean. His latter-day followers apparently see nothing ironic in this and carry on their master's tradition to this day. Another Zen group I checked out in LA offered expensive seminars at fancy hotels that promised instant enlightenment. Ain't no such thang as instant enlightenment. But we'll get to that.

The LA Zen scene wasn't all commercialized nonsense, though. I managed to find a few sincere places of Buddhist practice hidden away like a shiny new dime in a pile of dog vomit.

Zenshuji is the official arm of the Japanese Soto school in Los Angeles. They offer down-to-earth, nonsense-free zazen sessions several times a week. Another group I found was a Rinzai-affiliated organization that met on Sunday mornings at a café in Little Tokyo a couple of hours before it opened for business. Joshu Sasaki, a Rinzai monk who just celebrated his hundredth birthday, runs a temple in the city and a retreat center on nearby Mount Baldy.*

I began to wonder if I could fit into the SoCal Zen scene. I certainly didn't have the backing to set up my own temple, though, or the desire to do so, even if I had had the cash. Then I met Christine Buckley, a fan of my first book who worked at one of the big film production companies. She wrote to me when she heard I was coming to California and told me about Dr. Chris Chappel, a comparative religions prof at Loyola Marymount University. He and some like-minded colleagues had found a little house in Santa Monica just a couple of blocks from the beach. Their plan was to rent the house out to teachers of various spiritual disciplines who could then use the space to teach their stuff. Christine asked if I might be interested. I was. So she made the introductions.

Dr. Chappel liked what I was doing and asked me if I'd like to teach at the Hill Street Center. Like all the other teachers there, I'd have to pay a share of the rent, based on how much time I'd be using the space. But I was earning enough from Nakano Productions that I could afford to pay, even if the donations I got from attendees at my class didn't cover it. So I was in.

Dr. Chappel asked if I had a following. I said I really didn't know. My book was selling, my blog was getting plenty of hits. But I had no idea if that would translate into people actually coming to do zazen practice with me. I started on a Thursday night in early 2005. I think four people showed up. After a while I developed a

---

* Where Leonard Cohen studied! Sasaki was also an early teacher of my first teacher, Tim McCarthy.

little cadre of around ten or fifteen people who I could count on to show up regularly, though it was rare for all of them to show up on the same day. I usually peaked at about seven people. Sometimes less, occasionally more.

One day a small, intensely beautiful girl with a Betty Page haircut came to class. Her name was Leilani. The moment she stepped through the door at Hill Street Center I was enamored of her. Something in her dark, almond eyes spoke volumes. It was a kind of deep sadness, but not hopelessness. It was the kind of sadness I understood, and somehow I felt instantly connected to her. She was young, but I had the sense that she'd seen a lot and couldn't be fooled. Every time Leilani came to class I got a little thrill. I hadn't felt this way about any woman since I was a teenager. But I held my feelings in check. I was a married man, and Yuka, my wife, was plenty hot too.

After about a year, the person who'd previously been using the space on Saturday mornings moved on, and so I switched from Thursdays to Saturdays. I figured more people might show up on a weekend morning than on a weekday evening. I was wrong about that. The numbers have remained pretty consistent. In the three years I've been there I still max out at about ten people a week. That's fine. Just one sincere person is enough.

I had this weekly Zen gig going by the time my dad suggested the Zen Death Trip to Ohio. Yuka agreed to take over my Saturday morning class the week I'd be gone. So off I went to Dallas, hoping for the best but fearing the worst.

# CHAPTER 3

## DALLAS TO CINCINNATI

*I* remember the first time Yuka came to visit my parents' place in Flower Mound, Texas. We were eating breakfast, and all of a sudden we could hear Mom shouting. "I don't want to! Leave me alone!" Not that it was quite as clear as that. It was more like, "I da waddoo! Leemee lone!" She was yelling and screaming and carrying on as if she was being attacked by a crazed Mau Mau with a machete.*

After a few minutes my dad came out and smiled sheepishly at us. "I'm just in the bedroom torturing your mom!" he said cheerily before heading back. Later on he told us that she had bad days like this when she just didn't want to get out of bed. My mother was never a morning person even when she was well. These days getting her up in the morning was a challenge. And making this trip in the allotted time required getting started early.

When I'd last visited a couple of months before the Zen Death

---

* For three years in the seventies we lived in Nairobi, Kenya, where there really were machete-carrying former Mau Maus — though they were not crazed. But that was a long time ago.

Trip, Mom was in a pretty bad state. For most of the week I was there she gave no indication that she recognized me or that she was even aware I was around. She wasn't catatonic. She just didn't seem to register my presence, though she did register my dad's. On the fifth day she finally displayed some awareness that I was there. But not a lot.

This time she recognized me right away and gave me a hug. The hospice people my dad got through Medicare to help him gave her a big old hospital bed that could be bent into roughly the shape of an easy chair. This is where she spent most of her days. So getting a hug from Mom meant that you walked over to her bed, she stretched out her bony arms as far as she could, you bent down, and she clutched at you. It was a bit hit or miss. But somehow we made it work.

A few years ago my dad bought a giant, gas-guzzling van to accommodate Mom's wheelchair and all the other stuff he had to cart around whenever he drove her anywhere. He resented the fact that he got a huge tax break for buying such a wasteful mode of transportation. But he really needed the van, as well as the tax break.

So we loaded Mom in and set off on our long, long drive across the USA. I'd lived in big cities for so many years, I'd almost forgotten that so much of our nation is an endless stretch of countryside broken up by little pockets of chain stores and fast food restaurants.

Mom seemed genuinely happy to be with us, driving through the wilds of America. Mostly she just stared out the windows. But even doing that had to have been a hell of a lot better than sitting in that hospital bed staring at the damned TV all day.

We were all pretty exhausted by the time we made it to Nashville to spend the night. Sharing a hotel room with my parents was an interesting experience. Mom would sometimes start making that noise of hers in the middle of the night, a little more quietly than in the daytime, a muted version of her usual tortured howl. Dad would just sleep right through it. I suppose he'd done so a thousand nights before. This was Mom's equivalent of talking in her sleep. I wondered what the neighbors thought when they heard it, because they had to have. But we made it through the night and headed to Cincinnati the next day.*

The trouble began when we got to Grandma's place. It was immediately evident that Dad's idea of bringing my mom up to see Grandma did not seem like such a great plan either to Grandma or to my Aunt Sarah.** Sarah and Grandma worried that Mom's presence would upset the other residents at the convalescent home, not to mention Grandma herself. This pissed my dad off royally.

I could see both points of view. Dad had gotten so used to Mom he didn't really *get* just how disturbing her presence could be. On the other hand, like my dad, I also thought that anyone who got disturbed by her oughta just deal with it. We live in a society that supposedly cares for the sick and disabled. Yet when the same individuals who support these ideas are confronted with real-life sick or disabled people, they run away as fast as they can. It's hypocrisy of the highest order.

In Buddhism we often talk about finding the Middle Way between two extremes. People usually only think of this in terms of Buddha's decision to find the Middle Way between spiritual asceticism and materialistic gluttony. But it also applies to day-to-day situations. My solution would have been the Middle Way. Bring Mom in for a few minutes, visit a little, hoping she'd be quiet for most of that time, then take her back out to the car. I could stay there with her while Dad visited with Grandma, and then we could all go home.

But that solution never even made it to the discussion table. As

---

* In respect to the memory of my mom, she didn't make that noise of hers all the time, nor was she ever ill behaved. For the most part she was quiet and as content as anyone could be in her position. I truly admire her for that. It must have taken incredible discipline. Her noises were just her way of trying to interact with us. I just wish she could have found a different method of doing so. Because when she did make that noise it was extremely unnerving.

** Who missed having four years of perfect attendance at high school so she could come and see me when I was born. She won't let me forget that.

soon as he arrived, Dad called Aunt Sarah at work, and they immediately locked horns in a monumental shouting match over the telephone while I sat there trying my best to keep Mom distracted. This
was not easy, seeing as how Dad was there just three feet across the
room bellowing into the phone at his sister.

In the end we left Mom on a comfy chair in front of the TV at
Grandma's place and went to the nursing home without her. Mom
couldn't move much, so there wasn't any danger she'd hurt herself.
The only real problem was her loneliness. I always felt bad about
doing this kind of thing to her. But this was how Dad insisted on
dealing with her. He didn't leave her alone very often, and God
knows he needed to be on his own sometimes.

Things went okay at the nursing home. I guess. It was a strain
for Dad not to mention what had gone down earlier. When Grandma
brought it up herself, Dad just fumed and gave a polite, noncommittal response. Aunt Sarah showed up a couple of minutes after we
arrived. This made things even more awkward. But we went through
the motions of a civilized family visit. Then we went back to
Grandma's house, where Mom had slipped most of the way down
out of her chair, as she often did in those days. She was fine, but
there's no way she could have seen the TV. It was hard to tell if she
even cared anymore. But she was happy to see us back. Dad went
through his many-times-daily struggle to get her in and out of the
toilet. I helped as best I could.

The next day Dad had some business to attend to down in
Cincinnati. He told me how to take care of Mom's bathroom visits.
This was to be my first experience toileting my mom. Back when I
worked at the Summit County Board of Mental Retardation our
clients — who were called "consumers" for reasons I never understood — ranged from those with very mild cases of retardation to
highly disabled people who would never learn to speak. These "consumers" could not work at all and were kept busy with various inef-
fectual tasks supposedly intended to train them to work at the level

of those in the higher-level rooms. Many of these people had the same kinds of toileting needs my mom now did. So I'd already had some experience wrestling uncooperative full-grown adults of both sexes in and out of toilets, as well as changing their diapers and wiping their privates. Still, none of these people was my mom.

Mom did not like me taking her to the toilet. That was about all she could clearly convey. I think it surprised her I was doing it. But I talked to her like the grown woman she was — without talking down to her as if she were a child or a sick person. I told her Dad was away and I had to do this, that I wasn't any more psyched about it than she was, but that there wasn't any other choice. She seemed to accept that and cooperated as much as she could. We got through it two or three times that day.* At some point that afternoon Aunt Sarah came by. I'm not really sure why. As soon as Sarah entered the room, Mom started getting riled up. It was obvious Mom's agitation had something to do with Dad's phone call to Sarah the previous night. It was then that I realized Mom understood a whole lot more of what was happening than either Dad or I suspected. She definitely knew Dad had been arguing with Sarah. Maybe she even knew that the argument had been about her. She most certainly wanted to give Aunt Sarah a piece of her mind about it.

Sarah was oblivious. To her my mom's noises must have sounded like the incoherent raving of a crazy crippled woman. Mom continued for a long while as Sarah shuffled around doing whatever it was she was doing. I finally took my aunt aside and explained that Mom had been quiet and seemed happy until she arrived and that I thought this had to do with the argument the previous night on the phone. Sarah said she understood and went home. Mom got quiet again almost as soon as Sarah left. I can only imagine how frustrating it must have been to her not to be able to communicate even the simplest of ideas.

---

* Forgive me if I don't recount the details.

## CHAPTER 4

# MONEY CHANGES EVERYTHING

**W**hen my dad came back from Cincinnati he was livid. Not about the encounter with Sarah and Mom. I hadn't even told him about that yet. But all the stuff about my mom visiting Grandma the previous night had been percolating in his brain all day so much that he just had to vent. He wasn't going to take this anymore. We were getting out of there *right now*.

I wasn't about to disagree with him. He had been treated extremely badly by his mother and sister. Then there was the inheritance. My dad tried to enlist me on his side in that dispute. But I told him there was an old Buddhist saying that if someone wants to take something from you, you should give it to them. As far as I was concerned, if Grandma wanted to keep the money that badly, she could keep it. I didn't need it.

Money's weird stuff. We all live with it. We all use it. We all need it. But we have no idea that money is not a substance that exists in the world. Not to sound too new agey, but money is a kind of shared energy, a social construct we've evolved over tens of thousands of years to represent people's contribution to society. It's a system that went sour a very long time ago. An economist could tell you better about the various theories behind how and why this happened and what it means. But it's obvious to anyone with any sense at all that the economic system we have in place no longer does what it's supposed to and that it desperately needs fixing.

It's not my intention in this cheap little piece of paperback entertainment to try and present a plan by which our economic woes can be solved once and for all. But I will tell you that Buddhism will play a part in the eventual righting of the wrongs that have been committed to our economy and in the gradual equalization of it. Of this I am certain.

But here's how I looked at the prospect of inheriting my fair share of the big pile of money my grandpa left behind. On the one hand, it might sound pretty nice on paper. Grandpa had two children and four grandchildren. So let's say we divvied that money up fair and square into six equal portions, leaving Grandma out of the picture for now to make the math easier. I'd stand to get a check for fifty thousand smackers just for having had the pure dumb luck of being the grandchild of a guy who never spent any of his money. Nice pay for doing nothing.

But everything "free" comes with a price. The price is equal to the value of that free thing. That fifty thou wouldn't be any more "free" than an equal amount of moola that I had to put in hours and weeks and months and years of labor to earn.

Everything you have, whether it's money or stuff, is an obligation. It is as much your duty to care for and nurture any object you own as it would be if that object were your child. All possessions come with responsibilities. More possessions equals greater responsibility. This is why Buddha advised his followers to own only those things they absolutely needed to sustain them. These days few Buddhists practice the extremes of poverty he advised. I certainly do not. But to the extent that I ignore Buddha's advice, I suffer.

It's possible that, in a society that produces so much more than the society of Buddha's day could have dreamed possible, it may be okay — perhaps even necessary — to own a bit more than the monks did twenty-five hundred years ago. As members of an economically based society we have a certain obligation to support and contribute to that society. So I think it's fine for contemporary Buddhists — even if they're monks — to live a decent life and to have some cool stuff. But we've got to be careful what we want. It's never useful or happy-making to desire too much.

Greed is very dangerous. Sometimes we think we can allow ourselves to have just a little bit of greed. But it never works that way. This truth is inherent in the very nature of greed. Greed is wanting more than you need. A little bit of greed always grows into a lot. Always and forever, without exception. I'm sorry to be so didactic. But it just does. Observe this closely for yourself during your zazen practice and you will see it.*

Sometimes people are greedy for money for causes that they consider "worthy." Dad wanted that money so he could help my mom. He deserved it. But the problem of greed doesn't depend on whether or not the motivations are pure, or even on whether or not you deserve the thing you desire. You can't have something you don't work for, no matter how you plan to use it. In the case of getting Grandpa's money, the required work was to battle with the members of our own family, an activity that made everybody involved miserable. There was no sense in entering such a battle.

To get back to the story, Dad wanted to go *right now*. Right now being already dusk, I wasn't quite as keen as he was on getting on the road. Maybe he was used to pulling all-nighters on the American highways, but I wasn't. I'm not a night person to begin with, and I could just see me getting sleepy while driving and us ending up in a gully in the middle of some highway in Kentucky. I told Dad about

---

* You are doing daily zazen practice, aren't you? Otherwise there's not much point to reading this book.

my conversation with Sarah. She wouldn't be back that night, and we'd have the place to ourselves. We decided to set off first thing in the morning.

The trip back to Dallas was thankfully uneventful. I learned that Subway has the best bathrooms for handicapped people and that my dad kind of likes Black Sabbath. When it came up on my iPod he commented on how cool it sounded. For a guy whose musical tastes mainly run to Willie Nelson, that was a surprise. Mom liked the X-rated comedy channel on the van's satellite radio.

Listening to her laugh at dirty jokes I didn't know she could even understand anymore, I remembered the trip we all took to Roswell, New Mexico, some months earlier. I'd been invited to give a talk at the Las Cruces Zen Center, and Dad arranged to come by and take me to Roswell with him afterward on some business he had there. Mom was with him, and all three of us visited the UFO museum there. Dad fell asleep in the lobby right by the big plaster of paris flying saucer, and Mom thought that was hilarious. She still laughed just like she had before she got so sick.

Sadly, though, the times Mom laughed were becoming fewer and farther between. She never complained of pain or discomfort. But her condition had to hurt. She couldn't even scratch herself any-more or tell someone where she itched. Her stiff muscles must have ached terribly.

We made it back to Dallas all right, and I said my good-byes and headed back for Los Angeles. LA wasn't really home as far as I was concerned, but for now it was all I had.

## CHAPTER 5

# DOES REAL BUDDHISM EXIST IN THE WEST?

*I* wrote my first book, *Hardcore Zen*, believing it wasn't even publishable. Who wanted to read the story of an ex–punk rock bass player and employee of a company that made cheesy Japanese monster movies who became a Zen master without ever giving up his punk-rock attitude or love of crappy films about giant lizards eating Yokohama? But apparently some people did. I started getting requests to speak at various Zen centers, colleges, and bookstores in the States and Canada almost immediately. But I was living in Japan at the time, and nobody wanted to pay plane fare, so that was that. Now that I was in America again I could accept some of these offers. And I'd be able to answer the question myself: does real Buddhism exist in the West?

When I started studying Zen in Ohio nobody wanted to know. Zen was hippie stuff. This was the eighties! It was all about mullets and family values, and Kajagoogoo. Zen? Who had time for that old shit? My generation wanted to snort coke and make money. Greed was good.*

---

* Have I mentioned how much I hated the eighties?

In the time I'd been away in Japan, though, Buddhism had become all the rage in America. But the stuff I'd been reading on the Internet and in magazines, and the things I'd been hearing from Americans who came to my Zen classes in Tokyo, had me wondering just what it was they were calling "Buddhism" back in my homeland. Much of it seemed absolutely unrelated to anything I had devoted myself to studying and practicing for two decades.

There were obvious rip-offs I couldn't believe anyone would fall for.* There were teachers who prattled on and on with cartoony sounding descriptions of heightened awareness that sounded like stuff from bad sixties acid-trip movies. Then there was the growing movement to bring back the idea that psychedelic drugs could give you in a single dose the insight that dedicated Buddhist practitioners spent decades working on. Buddhism in America sounded like a complete catastrophe.

But my first Zen teacher, Tim McCarthy, was an American, and what he taught and practiced wasn't so different from what I'd been pursuing in Japan. Tim couldn't have been the only decent Zen teacher in the entire Western hemisphere. Real Buddhism *must* exist elsewhere in the West. Yet it seemed like the media were chasing after tawdry fantasies promoted by charlatans in pretty robes instead. I started thinking maybe I'd go seek out real Buddhist practice in the United States and Canada and use my new position as some kind of low-rent celebrity to try and bring some of that to light instead.

My travels around the country to talk to people about Buddhism have convinced me that although there *are* scam artists calling themselves Buddhist teachers out there in the wilds of the wild, wild Western world, they are the exception, not the rule. Most people who hang their shingle as Buddhist teachers are at the very least sincere and well-meaning and at best the kind of people who go entirely

---

* Zen Master Rama, the guy I talked about in a previous chapter who taught "Tantric Zen," whatever the hell that is, for example.

unrecognized during their lifetimes but will be regarded as saints and foreseers of the future of humankind by generations as yet unborn. Go find one and make friends.

But some of the scams that do exist ought to be mentioned. I'm not going to name any specifically, because that's just a big pain in the ass. Besides, I don't want to inadvertently send any business to the guys I want to talk about. But some general trends in Western Buddhism are pretty dire.

One of the worst is the idea that there are ways to speed a person to enlightenment. In the thirteenth century it took Dogen weeks to travel from Japan to China. Nowadays we can get halfway across the world in a matter of hours. Naturally, then, what took guys like Dogen decades to figure out, we should be able to realize in minutes. This is the twenty-first century, after all.

This sounds logical, but it's the wrong analogy. A better one would be to compare gaining enlightenment to gaining physical fitness.* You can't build up a bod like Arnold's in *The Terminator* any faster now than you could a thousand years ago. Some things never change, and never will. I'm sorry if you don't like that, but it happens to be true.**

There are, unfortunately, a lot of guys out there hawking instant enlightenment scams. According to one of these people, his trademarked technique will give you an authentic *kensho* or *satori* experience in which you realize your True Nature just like Buddha did under the Bodhi Tree in a single half-day session. I am not exaggerating, I swear. According to his own literature you will have yours "before lunchtime." Which is good because you never want to awaken to the true nature of yourself and the universe on a full stomach. You might get a cramp.

---

\* You don't really *gain* enlightenment, but I'll use that word just to make the connection.
\*\* Actually I'm not sorry. Sorry!

This, of course, is pure horseshit. But there is so little under-standing of what *kensho* or *satori* — enlightenment, in other words — actually is, that he and plenty of others can get away with this kind of malarkey. It's not easy to explain what enlightenment is. So let me start off by trying to explain what it isn't.

Enlightenment is not a cool experience you have, which you then file away with all your other cool experiences. It's not like that acid trip you took at Burning Man five years ago or that really wicked bike ride down an active volcano in Hawaii when you were in college. It's certainly not something you can buy for less than it costs you to hire a hooker,* then clean up and go get lunch. It's also not some-thing that someone who's gotten can now give you.

In Dogen's lineage we talk about two kinds of enlightenment. Dogen famously said that zazen is enlightenment itself. Sitting on your cushion and doing zazen is the actual enlightened activity of Buddha. So enlightenment for Dogen was not some experience you had. It was an activity you did.

The practice of zazen is unassailable. It doesn't matter what you think. It doesn't matter what you feel. It doesn't matter if you hate it or love it. It doesn't matter if you think you're doing it wrong and wasting your time or if you're all jazzed up about how cool and "Zen" you are. The practice itself transcends all attempts to box it in.

There's a story in which a Zen master hears about a wandering monk who says, "If a clear mind comes, let it come. If a cloudy mind comes, let it come." The Zen master grabs him and yells, "What if neither a clear mind nor a cloudy mind comes?" The monk says, "I hear they're having a big sale on underwear at JC Penney"** and wanders off. The master says approvingly, "I *thought* this was no ordinary monk!"

There's also another kind of enlightenment. When you've done

---

* Um, so I've heard.
** Okay. He actually says something about the marketplace. But it's basically the same meaning. The monk was having none of the intellectual discussion.

the practice of zazen for years and years you begin to accumulate little bits of understanding. At some point these little bits and pieces begin to come together. Gradually a kind of deeper intuitive knowledge starts to form. At some point this process reaches a kind of threshold and there may be a single moment in which everything seems to change. Or maybe several of those moments. Or maybe none at all, just a sense that something has changed.

That doesn't mean that everything gets fixed forever. You still have to live, with all the hassles you had before. You just have a better idea about what it is you're living and how to deal with it. That doesn't mean you'll always do what you should, though. Enlightenment has to be practiced.

The first kind of enlightenment happens instantaneously, as soon as you sit on your cushion. You can put this book down and go have it right this second.*

As for the second type, there is no way to get it without years of practice. That's just the way it is. And nothing will ever change that. No miracle drug. No miracle process. Nothing. Imagining you could get enlightenment quickly would be like imagining you could do fifteen minutes of sit-ups and get a bod like one of the chicks from *America's Next Top Model*, or thinking you could take a single guitar lesson and emerge playing Eddie Van Halen's "Eruption," or believing you could take one yoga class and be able to bend your leg around the back of your head afterward. It just doesn't happen that way. Never can. Never will.

But since there's no real understanding among the general public of what this enlightenment stuff is, anyone can claim that just about anything is enlightenment and a lot of people will believe it.

---

* There must be a zillion websites with instructions on how to do zazen — my own blog, hardcorezen.blogspot.com, has some with one of the Suicide Girls (we'll get to who they are in a bit) demonstrating, or you can buy a copy of my first book, *Hardcore Zen*, and find them in the last chapter — ch-ching!

What that waste of space who invented the wicked-cool enlightenment-in-an-hour process has stumbled on is nothing more than a way to hypnotize folks and give them a really tripped-out cool experience. He then tells them this experience is enlightenment, and since he's supposed to be a Zen master they believe him. He walks away with a few thousand bucks, and all the suckers leave feeling pretty good about themselves. No harm done, right?

Well, actually, no. In fact, this kind of thing can cause a whole lot of damage.

To show you why, let me ask you something. What do you imagine happens to a guy who gets a wild tripped-out dissociative experience in an afternoon and has some other person who's supposed to be a "spiritual master" interpret that experience for him as enlightenment just like Buddha's? How does the guy feel about the master who he thinks gave him this great gift? Does he owe the master something now? And will the guy do pretty much anything the master asks him to just so the master will keep on confirming the guy's enlightenment? What if the guy does something the master doesn't like and the master starts telling everyone the guy isn't enlightened anymore? Does the guy's enlightenment even exist without the master's confirmation? That's a key question. And, for bonus points: Having just parted with a hundred and fifty smackers, is the guy a) more or b) less likely to admit he's been ripped off? Answers on a postcard, please.

People love to be told they can get a big payoff with no real investment. But when was the last time you got something for nothing?

Here's another way the fast track to enlightenment stuff causes real damage. A Zen teacher friend told me the story of a woman who went to Japan to study in a Zen temple that emphasized having enlightenment experiences as quickly as possible. This was a far more traditional setting than one of those instant-enlightenment seminars. Which means they wanted you to get enlightened in a couple of weeks instead of in an hour.

This woman happened to be going through some pretty heavy shit in her life at the time she went to the temple — something like a divorce or a lingering illness in the family, that kind of thing. Add to that the culture shock of just coming to Japan and the triple culture shock of living in a Zen temple and the quadruple culture shock of being a white woman in an all-male Japanese Zen temple, and you have a surefire recipe for a nervous breakdown.

And that's exactly what happened. The poor woman started cracking up under the stress. Only her teachers told her that this was a sign that she was about to experience enlightenment, if only she pushed a little harder. So she pushed harder for her big breakthrough. And boy, did she get it. She went completely wacko and finally had to be forcibly ejected from the temple. It took her years to get over it. God only knows what kind of things some of the victims of those instant-enlightenment seminars are going through now.

There's a truckload of extremely good reasons why you don't want to rip open the doors of your subconscious too quickly. If you're not fully prepared for what's behind those doors, they're better left shut tight until such time that you are. It's a dangerous game to fuck with people's heads.

In the furious-paced, get-it-done-yesterday world we live in, the idea of In-N-Out Enlightenment sounds pretty appealing. But do you really think someone who weasels you in with an appeal to your hunger for big experiences right away so you can move on to the next thing has anything of value to offer? It is this very hunger for big experiences that real Buddhist practice is intended to root out.

Buddhist practice is difficult and takes a lot of time, effort, and energy. I know no one likes hearing that. But tough titty if you don't. There are no shortcuts. There are no easy ways to circumvent the pain and difficulty of practice any more than there are ways to develop a hot bod without working out for years. But you know what? It's not really *that* painful or difficult. You just sit on a cushion and stay still for a little while every day. If you can't handle that much effort, I feel pretty bad for you.

As Buddhism becomes more widely accepted, guys trying to make a fast buck on people's misconceptions about it are going to keep crawling out of the manure. It's really a buyer-beware situation. If you think enlightenment is something someone can give you in a big hurry for $150, you deserve what you get. But if you're ready to face reality, the real practice is there, and the real teachers are more plentiful than you can imagine.

Let me tell you about one of the places I went where they had real practice but were looking for someone to give them a bit of direction.

## CHAPTER 6

# THE ABUSE OF POWER IN ZEN, OR WHAT HAPPENS WHEN A ZEN MASTER SLEEPS WITH HIS STUDENTS

*I*ncredibly enough, Minnesota is kind of a hotbed of Zen Buddhism these days. Shunryu Suzuki, the author of *Zen Mind, Beginner's Mind* and probably the person most responsible for bringing real Soto-style Zen practice to America, had two main assistants when he was head of the San Francisco Zen Center. One was Dainin Katagiri, and the other was Kobun Chino. Kobun Chino would later become the teacher of my first teacher, Tim McCarthy. Katagiri was the one who turned Minnesota into a hotbed of Zen.

The legend goes like this. One time Suzuki was traveling with Katagiri across the country for some reason or another. The plane they were on happened to make a stop at the Minneapolis airport. When they were in Minneapolis, probably wandering through the airport to get to their connecting flight, Suzuki turned to Katagiri and said, "If you want to teach Zen to Americans, you should come to a place like this." Meaning that Minneapolis was the real America, unlike San Francisco, which is a humongous coastal city with a large Asian population and progressive attitudes quite unlike those in the rest of these here United States.

Sometime after Suzuki died, Katagiri decided to heed his advice. He packed up his belongings and moved to Minneapolis to start a new life out there in the land of Prince and Hüsker Dü and the Replacements. In the following years he established several Zen centers in Minnesota, including the Minnesota Zen Center in Minneapolis, the Hokyoji Retreat Center in southern Minnesota, and Clouds in Water Zen Center in St. Paul. Nice work.

Now, the people at the Clouds in Water told me they were looking for a new "guiding teacher." As part of the process they were inviting a number of teachers to their center to sort of audition for the role. One of the people they wanted to invite was me. The fools! Not that they're foolish people in general. But me? A guiding teacher? I don't know what they were thinking. But who am I to turn down a free trip to Minnesota?

I was originally contacted by a guy named Marc Anderson. He's a percussionist, and his hands are fat with giant calluses from playing conga drums for days on end. He put me up in the spare room of his groovy St. Paul pad. The Clouds in Water Zen Center is housed in what looks like a disused factory or warehouse down near the river. Once you get through the big industrial doors, though, the interior is set up just like a genuine Zen temple.

I got an earful when I asked why Clouds in Water was looking for a new leader. A lot of people seemed to want to talk about what had happened. I don't remember the whole story. Suffice it to say there was trouble, and the trouble stemmed from real or perceived sexual indiscretions of their former teacher, and the net result was that he was booted out. He was a married monk who had an affair with one of his students, an all-too-common story.

When a scandal like this takes place, our usual sense is that one bad spiritual leader-type person does nasty sexual or otherwise inappropriate stuff to a group of nice followers who then realize what's going on and kick him out for being such a bad guy. But this is never what really happens. When stuff like this goes on, the entire community contributes to it. Always.

In the case of the various guru sex scandals that seem to pop up with alarming regularity, it usually goes like this. A charismatic, or at least reasonably cool, person draws a group together around him.* A community forms, and that person becomes their master. Maybe he wants to be the leader of the group. Maybe he just accepts it as inevitable. In either case, someone's got to be the head of the organization and — tag! — he's it. The community then proceeds to foist all their expectations, dreams, and general fantasies about what a Great Enlightened Master ought to be like onto this unfortunate person. The image they create is absolutely impossible for anyone to live up to.

Too often the spiritual leader will try his best to be what his followers expect him to be. He may do so because he's full of himself and truly believes he's God's gift to the world. But usually that's not the case. We all want to please others and be liked — including those among us who end up in the position of spiritual teachers. When you find yourself surrounded by people who want you to be whatever they envision a "perfected master" to be, it's hard to tell them you're not. It feels mean. Even though the kindest thing you can do is to demolish their dreams, you really don't want to make them unhappy or make them dislike you. So a lot of well-meaning guys end up trying their level best to be the impossible thing their followers seem to want. This is where the trouble starts.

In trying to be what he's not — what nobody is or can ever hope to be — our unfortunate spiritual master gradually begins to lose balance. As he strives to be a spiritual superman, the scales tip farther and farther. His mind and body are soon way out of whack,

---

* Or her, but please don't make me repeat that over and over; we'll just assume our example guru person is a man, since men get themselves in deep shit over this kind of stuff more often than women.

and he begins to lose whatever grip on reality he might have had to begin with.

Soon enough the balance needs to be restored. At this stage our guru begins secretly trying to undermine his followers' unrealistic beliefs in him even while simultaneously trying to live up to them. He generally does not do this consciously or deliberately. But often such unconscious drives are far stronger than the ones we're aware of. Thus he becomes in private just as sinister as his public image is saintly.

Or else he may be completely open about these weird activities, explaining to his followers that shagging his students or stockpiling guns or taking copious amounts of cocaine or whatever he's doing is a special manifestation of his deep wisdom, or some such thing.

If he decides to be open about his indiscretions, the smaller community around him may tolerate it for a time. But the larger community will not. Then you get something like the Branch Davidians or Aum Shinrikyo, where the larger community descends on the smaller one and demolishes it.

But usually it doesn't go that far. What normally happens at this stage is that the followers our guru has gathered around him desperately try to hang on to their fantasy of the "perfected master," even in the face of overwhelming evidence their guy ain't it. It's hard to admit you were wrong, especially about something you probably insisted to everybody you knew was a divine truth. Maybe you even gave your car and your house and your girlfriend to him. How can you now say the guy was not The Guy? Plus, there's even a chance that it wasn't just that you were wrong about the guy you've been following. Maybe there's no such thing as a perfected master at all. That would ruin everything. So there's a lot at stake here on the followers' side as well. They'll tolerate just about anything to avoid facing up to the facts, even when those facts become unmistakably clear.

This whole thing is a big dilemma for anyone in the Zen master business. I've seen for myself just how much students will project onto their teachers. It's tremendous pressure. I've met students who desperately wanted me — me! — to fulfill their wild fantasies of the spiritual superman. When I first took on the role of Zen teacher I started getting massive headaches as a result of struggling with the many expectations that were suddenly foisted on me.

I understand the pressure of trying to be a leader to a group of people, many of whom are desperate to defer the responsibility for their own actions onto you. One of the basic human desires is the desire to be dominated. Dictatorships and cults arise from the desire of certain communities to be dominated by some powerful figure. Our primate relatives often live in small packs dominated by one unquestioned leader. Maybe this is how we're programmed to respond. In any case, a dictator doesn't come into power by his personal force alone. He comes into power when people want to be led, when people want to transfer responsibility onto some supposedly greater person.

It's very convenient to be told what to do. You no longer have to think for yourself. You no longer have to make your own decisions. That can be a tremendous relief. It's why some of the smartest people in the world often fall prey to the kookiest cults. They're just tired of being responsible for themselves.

Students are every bit as accountable as their teachers when this kind of nastiness goes down. As students we have to learn not to expect our teachers to be more than human. Much as we may want to believe that they are some kind of superior being, we have to put that fantasy aside.

You may be thinking that if a Zen master isn't able to withstand a bit of pressure from his students he's not a very good Zen master. Well, okay, sure. It would be wonderful if everyone who ever received dharma transmission* were strong enough to handle whatever got heaped on him by his students. But Zen is a philosophy for

---

* That's the ceremony in which a Zen teacher officially grants a student permission to teach in their lineage.

the real world. And in the real world even Zen masters sometimes aren't that strong.

Anyway, as part of Clouds in Water Zen Center's process of auditioning potential new guiding teachers to replace their disgraced former master, they developed a list of questions to determine whether or not the candidates were worthy. Here's one that relates well to what we've been discussing:

*What are the most important ways to guard against abuse of power in the relationships that must develop between a teacher and students or within other sangha relationships?*

One way to guard against abuse of power as a student is never to give your own power away. If you find you have done so, try taking it back and see what happens. If it isn't given back freely, there is something wrong.

A good Zen teacher will toss the power you attempt to hand him right back at you like a hot potato. For the student this is extremely frustrating. When my teachers threw the power I tried to give them back to me, I hated it. *Hated it.* In *Hardcore Zen* I talked about a profound mystical experience I presented to Nishijima, asking him if it was enlightenment. He told me I watched too many cartoons. Ouch! But had he verified that experience as enlightenment, what would have happened? The verification itself would have been my giving up my power to him. After all, I couldn't decide if what I'd experienced was real or not, but he could. From then on I would have been wholly dependent on him. What I really wanted wasn't enlightenment. I wanted desperately to find someone who would take my power from me so that I could relax and let them take the blame for everything. This whole abuse of power thing gets down to what it really means to be a Zen teacher. So I'd like to talk about that a little.

It hasn't been that long since religious authority figures in the West stopped being something akin to policemen. There are still a lot of places where the two are almost the same. Like policemen, religious teachers are given their authority by the people they serve. The people are the boss.

But policemen don't serve by doing what is asked of them on command, like waiters or butlers. They serve by upholding rules and regulations the society has decided on. In enforcing these rules they often have to act in ways individual members of society find uncomfortable or restrictive. They hand out traffic tickets, they blow whistles at you when you cross against the light, and in extreme cases they are even empowered by society to kill you. In the same way, we allow religious authority figures to chastise us for breaking spiritual rules. In some religions, the authority figures may even mete out punishment — seven Hail Marys and two How's Your Fathers for masturbating on a Sunday or whatever. In some countries religious authority figures can even kill you for breaking God's law.

Even if we haven't memorized the law books of our state, we all have a pretty good idea of what a policeman should and should not do. In the same way, even if we're not Catholic or Jewish we have a fairly clear idea of what a priest or rabbi should and shouldn't do. We may be a little vague on the details. But overall we kinda know. If you saw a Catholic priest hanging out at a strip club or a rabbi at a race track you might feel inclined to question him, even if you weren't a member of the faith.

When setting up the early Buddhist sangha, Gautama Buddha saw the problems of religion and religious authority very clearly. He was aware of issues like the abuse of power and the mindless worship of ancient texts. But in setting up his organization he saw there were some useful aspects to the organized religious structure that should not be thrown away. So Buddhist monks dressed and acted like monks were supposed to dress and act. They served their sangha in many of the same ways that religious authorities in the past had. Yet these monks and teachers were something altogether different from what religious authority figures had been before.

Rather than being a religious authority, a Zen teacher* is more like some kind of strange performance artist. An artist needs to be attentive to the needs and wants of his or her audience. But an artist's most important commitment is to the truth. An artist needs to express what is true, whether or not that truth makes the audience uncomfortable, and whether or not it's what the audience wants or expects to see or hear.

To some degree we also need to be role models. But this does not mean what it is usually taken to mean. I think our usual sense of what a role model does is that he presents a highly idealized version of how to behave. People who aspire to be role models try very hard to hide any aspect of their personality that might be judged as negative. But this never works very well. Eventually the flaws are brought into the open, often in shocking and spectacular ways. It seems the more folks try to hide their foibles, the more shocking such revelations are.

A Zen role model needs to be very open. Zen teachers have to expose their flaws as well as their graces. That's not always easy because we want to hide those things. And we certainly don't want anyone to imitate them! Of course Zen teachers do need to cultivate a state in which we do fewer of the things we wouldn't want anyone to imitate. But we still have to be open about those aspects that aren't so nice. Confused people may imitate those things, it's true. But that can't really be helped.

The folks in St. Paul had a lot more questions I won't go into

---

* I tend to use the words *monk* and *teacher* somewhat interchangeably. All Buddhist monks are, in some sense, teachers of Buddhism. But one of the definitions of dharma transmission is "permission to teach." Not all monks are dharma transmitted. In some Zen institutions there are specific designations and levels. Certain monks are allowed to teach, while others can perform ceremonies but are forbidden to teach. My own lineage did not make these kinds of clear distinctions. Everyone Nishijima gave the precepts to was encouraged to teach if they desired to. Those who received dharma transmission weren't just encouraged to teach but expected to. I do not claim this lack of clear delineation makes us better, just different.

here. I had a good time there. But ultimately they didn't want me to
be their guiding teacher. This was fine by me because, as much as I
liked them and their place, I didn't really think I'd do so well as their
leader. Besides, I still wanted to do the stuff Nakano Productions
sent me to Los Angeles to do.

At the same time as I was doing all this running around and jab-
bering about Buddhism, my wife, Yuka, was acclimating to life in
America far better than I was. While I was happy to travel and glad
to be able to spend time with my family, I wasn't too jazzed up about
being back living in the good ol' US of A. I'd left America because
I hated America. My feelings had eased up a little in the eleven years
since I'd last lived here. But not that much. I still wasn't a huge fan
of the place. And I found Southern California as vapid and superfi-
cial as any Woody Allen movie had ever portrayed it. I had to be
there to do what the company I worked for wanted me to. If not for
the job, though, I would never have lived in Los Angeles.

Yuka, on the other hand, loved it. To her everything about LA
was exciting and new, a grand adventure in an exotic land. Within
her first year of working in America she'd been promoted to manager of the Beverly Hills location of a world-famous retail chain and
had turned the place from being a money loser to one of the company's top stores. But to the extent that America held new excite-
ment and adventure for her, she began to find her American husband
more and more passé and boring, obsessed with his newfound role as
Zen teacher to the masses and harried by the increasing difficulties of
being the American liaison for a company whose already dire troubles seemed to be deepening by the day and worried sick about his
parents.

In spite of my initial enthusiasm, my job started to get very
weird, and not in a good way. Two months after I'd packed up eleven
years of my life and moved it across the Pacific Ocean for Nakano
Productions and Zone Robo, I got word that both the president and
the vice president of the company — the men who'd hatched the

plan to send me to the States — had been fired. Mind you, I did not receive any official notification of this. In fact, to this day I still haven't. I had to hear it from a fellow employee who assumed I already knew. Then the new management told me they'd decided to close their Los Angeles office. Communications were so strained that it took me two weeks to finally work out that what they meant by this was that they'd decided to close the physical office space they'd been renting for me in Century City and have me work out of my apartment. At least I still had a job. For now.

But worries about work soon gave way to more pressing matters.

## CHAPTER 7

# MY MOM IS DEAD (AND SHE'S NOT GONNA TAKE IT ANYMORE)*

*I*n December 2006 Yuka, my sister, her kids, my sister's new husband, and I all went to Dallas to celebrate Christmas with my mom and dad. Actually, we ended up getting there a day or two after the day itself, which was better anyhow, since travel was cheaper and easier. None of us was all that fussed about doing Christmas exactly on the 25th anyway. We've never been a religious family.

My sister Stacey's first husband was Jewish, so when he was around Christmases became even more secular. Stacey and Dave had gotten divorced a couple of years earlier. Of their two children, Ben, who turned seventeen that year, had decided to embrace his Judaism in a big way.

Stacey's daughter, Skylar, who was ten at the time, had chosen to lean toward Christianity like her mom. They liked to attend the local Baptist church together. But while Stacey considered herself a Baptist,

---

* This title refers to a Cleveland band fronted by Mark Edwards called My Dad Is Dead whose first album was titled "And He's Not Gonna Take It Anymore." They're great. My band Dimentia 13 recorded its never-to-be-released fifth album at Mark's recording studio, the Beat Farm.

I suspect her take on the faith probably wasn't quite like that of the other parishioners. I remember having a conversation with her in which I said that I couldn't really understand the whole obsession many American Christians had these days with proving the Bible was historically accurate. If Christianity is really meaningful, I said, it should have just as much meaning even if someone invented a time machine and went back and discovered that Jesus never really existed. To my surprise she agreed with that idea and even liked it.

This was going to be the first time I was to spend any extended amount of time with Stacey's new husband, Ronnie, a burly ex–military man. I was wary of him at first, since my early childhood encounters with macho types had been uniformly negative. But while we were there he displayed an impressive knowledge of deeply geeky *Star Trek* trivia. Maybe he was okay after all.

My mom's condition hadn't deteriorated too much since the Zen Death Trip. But that's not saying a lot. Still, she recognized and interacted with all of us. It wasn't clear if she knew it was Christmas or if she understood the presents we were giving her. But she certainly knew she was with her loved ones, and that was nice.

At one point we got everybody together for our annual family portrait. A number of years ago, during a family get-together, we noticed it was pretty unfair that whoever set up the camera's timer had to run into the shot while everybody else stayed posed. So we started a tradition of everyone standing behind the camera so that we'd all have to run into the shot and be just as flustered as the cameraman. As Mom's condition worsened we'd give her a head start or let her sit and laugh at us as we all scrambled for positions. Now Dad had to prop her up just to get her in the photo, so we gave up on everyone running into the shot and just did the photos the normal, boring way. This was to be our last family portrait with Mom in it.

Her condition was so bad that I remember sitting up in bed one night while we were there, thinking, "If only there was a way to end this misery for her quickly and painlessly." I caught myself short. Was I really contemplating murdering my own mother?

There is no official Buddhist stance on the matter of euthanasia. But if I can speak for myself rather than implicating the entire community, as a Buddhist I do not find the idea entirely objectionable. If a person wishes to die and someone close to him or her can handle making that happen, it's really not any of my business, and it's certainly not the government's business either. There is no sin involved either in the killing or in the decision to die. In Buddhism the concept of sin does not exist. Still, generally Buddhists tend not to want to interfere with the natural order of things. When Shunryu Suzuki and Dainin Katagiri were dying of cancer they did not ask their students to end their lives for them, nor did Dogen when he was dying at age fifty-four of what was most likely tuberculosis. I would imagine these men believed it was their duty to experience what life demanded they experience. And, when it came down to what I was and was not capable of doing for my mother, I could not kill her. At that point she could not clearly express her wishes in the matter. But had she been able to, I honestly cannot say what I would have done. I imagine I'd probably have found some way to do what she wanted.

So I did not kill my mom. Instead I spent time sitting quietly with her, feeling with a certainty I really can't describe that she'd be gone before January was over. After a few days with her and Dad, we all said our good-byes and went home. I didn't tell anyone, but I knew I'd never see my mom again. Somehow I think she knew it too.

My mom died sometime during the night of January 12, 2007. My dad put her to bed around midnight, and when he got up the next morning she was gone.

I woke up in the very early morning that day, maybe at 3:00 or 4:00 a.m., and in my head I heard John Lennon's song "My Mummy's Dead" from the Plastic Ono Band album. It played all the way through, very clearly, every word, every chord, from beginning to end. At the time I thought it was odd that song would come to mind, but it wasn't especially remarkable. I just peed and went back to bed.

I got a call at about 5 a.m. from my dad telling me my mom had died during the night.

So now I had to get my ass out to Dallas again and deal with all the stuff you have to deal with when your mom dies. Luckily my dad's not big on funerals, nor was my mom. Dad had already decided not to have one.

This was especially good for me because, being a priest or a monk or whatever the hell I am, I'm really the one who ought to have been doing the service. But I have no idea how to do a Buddhist funeral service. That probably strikes some of you nice people as weird. But it shouldn't.

It's only in more recent times that funeral services and the like have become an important part of Buddhism. Unfortunately, though, in Japan today, as far as most people are concerned, Buddhism *is* funeral services. Most Japanese people go to Shinto shrines for ceremonies related to birth and coming of age, to Christian churches — or at least places that sort of look like Christian churches — for weddings, and to Buddhist temples to get their funerals taken care of. So all those other religions are about birth and life, and the Buddhists, what with their black clothes and all that incense and everything, are only good for stuff having to do with death.

Though Buddhism wasn't always about death, Buddha himself must have participated in funeral services of some sort since a few of his closest followers died before the master himself bit the big one. But when his followers asked Buddha what they should do after he died, he told them not to worry about him, just to devote themselves to their practice. They went ahead and had a big-ass funeral ceremony for him anyway, though. Putzes.*

Dealing with the death of a loved one is never easy. Hypnotized robot zombies decked-out as "spiritual"-type people might be able to pretend it's nothing to get uptight about, man. But I'm not interested

---

* Or maybe he didn't say not to worry about him. An alternate account has Buddha telling his followers exactly how his big-ass funeral should be conducted. I favor the story in which he says not to worry. But it's possible that Buddha, being a realistic guy, knew his followers would have a big funeral anyhow and did give instructions on how it should be performed. He may indeed have said both things.

in numbing myself. In the real world, where I live, having your mom die hurts. It hurts bad.

But you deal with the things you gotta deal with until you can't deal with anything anymore. I'm not gonna pretend I just sailed through this thing all starry-eyed, going, "Life is death and death is life" like some kind of cartoon Zen master. It was tough. But I'm glad to have had the practice I've had and the insights it's given me into stuff like this because it helps. It really does.

You never know what's gonna come up in your life. When something big happens, like your mom dying, for example, you really don't know how you're going to react. This is why Zen guys do the practice of zazen.

Zazen is very different from what most folks think of as meditation. It's not goal oriented. You take your seated posture with your legs all twisted up just like you do in pretty much any meditative practice. But in a lot of those other practices you use that posture for some purpose. Maybe you're trying to reach enlightenment or raise your "serpent power," or what have you, up through your spine, or maybe you're just trying to find tranquility and peace of mind. I don't want to name the practices I'm thinking about here or give you the impression that I think they're uniformly bad. All I can say along those lines is that I've seen them and tried a few, and I'm just not interested. Zazen practice is very different. It has no goal. You do zazen in order to do zazen. But in this truly most stupid of all practices lies something very profound.

In a weird way we're always prepared for whatever we have to face. We just don't know it. We always have an intuitive sense of right action. But we're also very, very good at shouting so loudly over that sense that we may not be able to hear it when it functions. Zazen helps you learn to uncover the intuition you already have.

In *Shobogenzo*,* Dogen devotes a chapter to the subject of death.

---

* The title of a massive multipart work on Buddhism written by Dogen in the thirteenth century.

It's called "Shoji," which means "Life and Death." It's only two pages long, so I can quote most of it right here. Dogen says, "If a person looks for buddha outside of life and death, it is to be amassing more and more causes of life and death, and to have utterly lost the way of liberation. When we understand that only life and death itself is *nirvana*, there is nothing to hate as life and death and nothing to aspire to as *nirvana*. Then, for the first time, the means exist to get free from life and death."

He goes on to say, "To understand that we move from birth to death is a mistake. Birth is a state at one moment; it already has a past and will have a future. Extinction also is a state at one moment; it too has a past and a future. In the time called life, there is nothing besides life. In the time called death, there is nothing besides death."

Then he says, "This life and death is just the sacred life of buddha. If we hate it and want to get rid of it, that is just wanting to lose the sacred life of buddha. If we stick in it, if we attach to life and death, this also is to lose the sacred life of buddha."

Some religions tell us that the truth is to be found in eternal life, free from death. Dogen didn't believe that. For him there was no truth outside of life and death.

Also, in Buddhist terms death isn't just something that happens when you're sixty-five like my mom was or even eighty-five or ninety-five or a hundred and twenty-five years old. Death is happening at every moment. In a chapter called "Shukke Sudoku," or "Merits of the Monastic Life," Dogen says that each day consists of 6,400,099,180 mind-moments. In ancient India some believed that the smallest increment of time was something called a *kshanta**** or "mind-moment." It was said that a snap of the fingers took sixty-four *kshantas*. In one *kshanta* the entire universe appears and disappears.

It's a pretty radical view of time and a pretty radical view of

---

* Gesundheit.

death. In Buddhist terms you die 6,400,099,180 times a day! Though each moment is a separate entity, we have the illusion of continuity and of a permanent self that passes through all these moments. But Buddhists entirely reject the idea that this sense of self is real.

Even though there is no eternally permanent self, the present moment is eternal. Though they appear and disappear faster than we can ever possibly perceive, each of those 6,400,099,180 moments is *now*. Your real being is no different from the present moment. You are a manifestation of real time, a manifestation of now.

There's an old Buddhist story that tries to illustrate the futility of using our usual frames of reference to understand what death is. A Buddhist teacher and his student are at a funeral parlor standing in front of a coffin. The student taps on the coffin and asks, "Alive or dead?"

The teacher says, "I won't say."

The student says, "Tell me, or I'll beat the crap out of you!"

The teacher still insists he can't say. So the student wails on him and stomps out.

Years later the student is still studying Buddhism, but under a different teacher. He gets word that his first master has passed away. He and the new teacher are commiserating about this and he tells his new teacher the story about the day at the funeral parlor. The new teacher says, "Why don't you try asking me the question?"

So the student says, "Is he alive or dead?"

The teacher says, "I will never say."

This time the student gets it.

It's hard to say why he gets it the second time but not the first. But, for one thing, he's not really the same person anymore. Thousands of days, with their 6,400,099,180 mind-moments each, have passed between the two incidents. The universe has been born and destroyed hundreds of billions of times. The student has matured. The same answer that twisted his cranium up all those years ago now makes perfect sense.

It's also significant that no words were added to the second explanation. We usually think that when something is hard to understand, we need to add more and more and more words to explain it. Our civilization has produced mountains of words to try and satisfy this need. In the story the only thing that's needed are the very same words that were already spoken.

Anyway. So there I was, sitting up in bed at 5 a.m. with the phone in my hand, groggy, a little confused. My dad was on the other end sobbing. I tried to be comforting, strong, all the things you try to do. She was his wife. She was my mom. We both had a lot invested in the relationship. But she had been ill now for well over a decade. One thing was certain. She had been miserable, and now she wasn't anymore.

I was the first one to get to my parents' — well, now it was just my dad's place — in the northern suburbs of Dallas. My sister couldn't make it out right away, and neither could my wife. So it was just me and my dad.

We talked a lot that first day. My dad and I confessed to each other that we'd both had thoughts of ending Mom's life for her during those final days. Dad said that once, a few years earlier, before her condition had gotten so bad she couldn't talk anymore, Mom had asked him to finish it for her. "You have a lovely gun," she'd said. That wasn't actually true. My dad never owned a gun. But he knew what she meant. My mom called all kinds of things that she viewed as helpful or useful "lovely." She meant that Dad had the means by which to help her end her life. She was not in good enough shape to do it herself by that time. I was glad I wasn't the only one who'd had such thoughts.

And she sometimes had good days, even right up until the end. In fact, the last time I saw her she was having a lot of reasonably good days — "good" being a matter of degree, of course.

Dad had been feeding her handfuls of pills several times a day for years, all duly prescribed by doctors who thought they knew what was best for her. Some were supposed to make her muscles looser, some were to make her stool softer, a few were antidepressants, and some were our old pal Mr. Valium. She'd had that vacant junkie stare for a long time. Sometimes she'd emerge from her fog, but most of the time she was deep in a chemically induced retreat from reality.

By the end of Mom's final year my dad had taken her off most of the dope. The pills didn't seem to be doing her very much good by then anyway. So at Christmas she was clearer and more present than she'd been in a long time. Even all the weird noises she made that the antidepressants and tranquilizers were supposed to stop had settled down some.

Now that she was gone there were no more noises. Her bed had been taken away, and the area where it had sat had been cleaned. It was eerily like she'd never been there at all.

Like I said, my dad didn't want a funeral. But he did want some kind of tribute to Mom. I suggested we put up a *butsudan*. A *butsudan* is a thing you find in most homes in Japan. It's a special kind of miniature shrine that looks a little like a liquor cabinet or something. Inside you put a little figurine of Buddha, and in front you set pictures of your dead relatives. Then you can offer them incense or flowers or fruit, sometimes sake or even cigarettes if they liked to smoke or drink in life.

I called every Buddhist organization or Oriental-themed shop I could find in the greater Dallas-area phone book looking for a place that might sell *butsudans*, but I came up empty-handed. Just when I was about to give up I remembered that members of the Soka Gakkai International (SGI for short) sect use them.

SGI is that branch of Buddhism that my friend "Larry," the guy who made up the phrase Zen Death Trip, belonged to. Tina Turner, Orlando Bloom, and Kate Bosworth are involved in it as well these days. I knew from my time sharing a house with Larry that all members of SGI keep a *butsudan* in their homes in which they enshrine a copy of the Lotus Sutra. SGI is pretty popular, and I figured they must have a shop in Dallas that sold *butsudans*. I was right. So off we went to get us one.

At the shop I tried to avoid any questions about what I intended to do with the *butsudan* I was buying. If they thought I was one of them, I'd get out without any trouble. The second we got our receipt we snatched up the *butsudan* and hightailed it out of there.

Once we got home we stuck a little Buddha that my mom had bought when she visited Japan the first year I lived there inside and put a nice photo of Mom in front. That would be her memorial. No tombstone. No urn for the ashes.

Mom was officially gone. Or was she?

## CHAPTER 8

# WHERE DO WE GO WHEN WE DIE?

The Heart Sutra is a great catchall scripture. It pretty much lays out everything you need to know about Buddhism in one little poem. I wrote a whole chapter about it in *Hardcore Zen*, so I'll skip the long explanation here. But one part of the sutra goes:

All dharmas are marked with emptiness
They do not appear or disappear
Are not tainted or pure
Do not increase or decrease
Therefore in emptiness no form,
No feelings, perceptions, impulses, consciousness
No eyes, ears, nose, tongue, body, mind
No color, sound, smell, taste, touch, object of mind
No realm of eyes and so forth until no realm of mind consciousness
No ignorance and also no extinction of ignorance
And so forth until no old age and death and no extinction
of old age and death.

My sister and her husband arrived in Dallas first, then Yuka showed up a couple of hours later. We'd all only just returned to our own places from Dallas a few weeks before, so this represented a major expense for everyone involved. Stacey's kids stayed with their father. By then we'd set up the little *butsudan*, but we still needed some incense and candles to do the chanting ceremony even close to correctly. The only place we could find any incense was at a Hot Topic in the local mall. We avoided the one called Love on the Beach and went for a plain old sandalwood scent. We lit the incense and some candles Mom had bought for a dinner party ages ago that never happened and gathered around the *butsudan* as I chanted the Heart Sutra.

So there I was chanting all this stuff about there being no old age and death in tribute to my mom who'd gotten old and died. Was I just escaping into a bunch of comforting words? I don't think so.

The sutra reflects the Buddhist concept of time. As I mentioned before, the only real time as far as Buddhism is concerned is right now. Right now there is no old age or death because old age and death are descriptions of things as they are now when we compare them to things as they used to be. When you eliminate the comparison of things with how they used to be you can't talk in terms of old age or death anymore. We chant the Heart Sutra for the living, to give them solace, but without offering comforting fantasies of heaven and the afterlife.

But even though I wasn't thinking in terms of life eternal beyond the Pearly Gates, the week after my mother passed away I was very much concerned with where she went after she died. The question was troubling me so greatly that I consulted a number of experts who were supposed to know what became of her after she shuffled off this mortal coil. But none of them could tell me anything about where she was.

See, Dad decided to have her cremated. He was pretty distraught that first day, so he left the Flower Mound Family Funeral Home of Flower Mound, Texas, in charge of everything. I thought someone ought to be in attendance at the cremation, as is the custom in Buddhist countries. But when I called the funeral home they had no idea when and where the cremation was to take place. They said her officially designated doctor, Dr. Madhavi Thomas of Texas Neurology PA, was supposed to sign off on some paperwork or something. So I called her office, but no one was there. Then I tried her emergency number and got an answering service who said they'd deliver a message to the doctor and ask her to get back to me. But I never got a call. So I called the funeral home again. And again. And again.

I heard a lot of excuses from the funeral home about why they didn't know what was going on with my mom. But no answers. I called the caregivers who'd worked with her for the past six months, but they didn't know anything either, though they did put in calls to the funeral home, and the doctor too. By this time my wife and my sister and her family all had to go back home. So it was just me and Dad again. Dad was in no shape to deal with this. Besides, he's a notorious yeller-atter of bureaucratic fuckups, so I wanted to keep him as far away from this situation as possible.

Finally, my sister, who is a lawyer, called the doctor's office from her office in Knoxville. Using her married name and not mentioning her relationship to Mom, Stacey gave it her best lawyer stuff. Finally I started getting some answers. Unfortunately the answers mainly amounted to better-worded excuses. Nobody knew yet where the hell she was or what was going to happen to her next.

Which brings up a side point I'd like to make. Hey, America, stop with the frikkin' excuses already! One of the most valuable things I learned while I was in Japan was how to stop making excuses. Over there, making excuses for anything at any time under any circumstances is seen as unacceptably childish for anyone above the age of three. Even trying to explain that your car really did get hit by a falling redwood during a hurricane and an earthquake while your head was being set on fire by a team of crazed pastry chefs and that's why you were four minutes late for the meeting makes you look like a spoiled baby. You just stumble in there with your limbs in casts and your face all blackened by the fire, stammer your most sincere apologies, and then sit down and shut up.

But here in America everybody's just full of excuses. Enough, already! Tell me you don't know the answer, and then go out and try to find the answer. I do not want to hear a bunch of lame-ass reasons why someone else made it impossible for you to do what you were supposed to be doing. Okay? And I especially don't want to hear it when the subject in question is the whereabouts of my dead mother. Got it?

But you didn't want a rant about people making excuses. You wanted to know where people go when they die as told to you by a real live Zen master right here in a cheap-ass paperback book you bought on a whim because it had a funny title. Well, unfortunately, you seem to have me confused with someone dead. 'Cuz I don't know. And neither does anyone else who tells you they do, by the way.

So maybe my mom's in heaven or Krishna Loka or Valhalla, or maybe she's in paradise with her seventy-two virgins. I can't say. Until I finally got some answers a few days later, I couldn't even say whether she was still on ice or if she'd already been burned to cinders and shoved into a $75 cardboard box. (The Flower Mound Family Funeral Home actually charges $75 for a cardboard box for your dead loved one's ashes.)

Yet I do know where my mom went when she died. She didn't go anywhere. She's right here, typing this, reading this, getting confused after having read this as to what the hell the author was trying to say. That's because my mom was a manifestation of the eternal present. So am I. So are you. So's this book. So's the toilet you're sitting on while reading it.* There is nowhere for her to have gone. There's nowhere you can go after you die either. There's only here.

In Buddhism, we say that body and mind are one and the same.

---

* Stop that! You'll go blind!

When you say that, most people think you're taking the materialistic view that the seat of consciousness is in the brain. But that idea is just another assumption made by the human brain. The idea that the brain somehow produces the mind is a carryover from the older belief in the existence of the human soul. It still takes the point of view that consciousness is some kind of fixed entity that belongs to each individual. We've just moved the position of this imaginary object called "self" out of the heart and into the head.

But Buddha rejected both these views entirely. None of our ideas — none of them, no matter how good they are or how supported they are by authority or even research — absolutely *none* of our ideas can ever, ever, ever be reality. Reality is entirely beyond what you or me or Jesus or the Dalai Lama or any other great master or great deity or great book could ever come close to conceiving of.

Which is not to say that Buddhism rejects good science. Good science and reasonable philosophy are wonderful things. We need them. They help us lead better, more enjoyable, more productive, and happier lives. The computer I'm using to type this right now is the product of the application of good and useful science. Philosophies like pragmatism and existentialism have helped a lot of people in the West come closer to the understanding Buddha established long ago. But the final answers will never be found in science or philosophy, not even Buddhist philosophy. We have the answers with us all the time. The answer to what life is, is life itself. And the answer to what death is, is death itself. Don't turn away from your life and your death, or you'll miss out on everything. Don't try to escape into fantasies of a world beyond this veil of tears, or into depression on contemplating the empty void you think you'll experience once your neurons fire their last. You have no idea either way. And it doesn't matter.

Shit, even knowing what's going to happen doesn't mean you have any idea what it'll be like when it happens. As I sit here writing this very paragraph I know I'm going to be eating lunch in half an hour, then doing a lecture a few hours later. I have no idea what my lunch will taste like or whether my lecture will be a good one or a disaster. No matter what we predict for our futures, we're always wrong anyway. The only sensible thing to do is to live this life as it is right now. Leave what happens after you die till after you die.

## CHAPTER 9

# *I DON'T KNOW*

*I* finally got a call from the Flower Mound Family Funeral Home on Friday about two hours before I was supposed to get on a plane and head back to Los Angeles. The cremation, they kindly told me, was set for the following morning around nine. I hastily rearranged my travel plans and stayed over an extra night at my dad's.

A crematorium in Japan is a well-maintained, solemn place for saying your final farewells to your loved ones. The one in Flower Mound looked like a reconverted garage or maybe a waste disposal facility, which, I suppose, is what it really is. The floor was dirty concrete. There was nowhere to sit down. There was a big riding lawn mower sitting over to one side. My mom was in a lousy giant cardboard pizza box with the word *head* printed gruesomely on one end so the guys handling her could figure out which end was what. The thing they slid her into even looked kind of like a giant pizza oven.*

---

* Mom was the only person I've ever known who actually liked green peppers on pizza. Most people are okay with them if they're there, I guess. But my mom actually wanted them put on her pizzas. I should have put some green peppers on her as a tribute.

The people who worked at the place were standing around in jeans and flannel shirts. You'd think they'd make some kind of concessions to people who wanted to pay their last respects. But it looked to me like that idea had never come up before. Weird.

So they slid her into the big pizza oven and switched on the heat. I chanted the Heart Sutra again. While we stood there Dad told me he'd run out and bought her some underwear right after he realized she was dead. This was even before he called someone to take her away. She'd been incontinent so long he'd thrown away all her underwear, and he didn't want her to be wearing those damned Depends adult diaper things when she was taken away.

We stood there not talking for a while longer till we figured she was all burned away. Then we went out and had some breakfast at a place Mom used to like. I think she would've been happy to know we had been at the cremation to keep her company.

The death of your mom is one of the hardest things you can face. Yet it's something pretty much everyone has to deal with at some point, seeing as how most of us are considerably younger than our mothers. A lot of us imagine that dying must be the very worst thing that can happen to a person. Our philosophies, our movies, the stories we tell each other, and even our legal system all seem to be based on this assumption. But I wonder if it's always true.

Certainly it's usually better to stay alive than it is to die. But there are many cases when it is not. My mom had a very hard time of it her last few years. I felt like her dying when she did was for the best. The only alternative would have been years more of lying in a crappy hospice bed with a TV droning on in front of her. At some point every one of us will end up in a state where the best thing to do is to die. And when it's better to die, then death doesn't need to be seen as such a horrible thing. Obviously it's the end of something. But do we really know what that means?

I do not believe in heaven and hell, at least not in the conventional sense. When you're feeling balanced, that's heaven. When you're not, that's hell. Nor do I believe in an afterlife or in reincar-nation.* On the other hand, I know that human life isn't at all what most of us conceive it as. When looked at from one side, we are each individuals with our own lives and our own deaths. No one else in the entire universe will ever experience your life or your death. And yet, when viewed from the other side, none of us is in any way separate from one another or from the world we live in. My mom is dead, and yet the universe continues on. She was an integral part of the universe and still is. Where has she gone? I don't know. Am I contra-dicting what I said in the last chapter about knowing where she went? Damn straight, I am. Life is contradiction. Deal with it.

The words *I don't know* figure big in Buddhist philosophy. But most of us have a very hard time understanding these words because we're always in a rush to add something after them — some kind of qualifier intended to shield our egos from having to admit there are things beyond its grasp. When we say, "I don't know" we usually actually mean "I don't know, but I wish you'd tell me" or "I don't know, but maybe if I study the matter hard I'll know." Our teachers, our parents, and our friends make us feel foolish and inadequate if we answer, "I don't know" to their many questions. But the Buddhist "I don't know" is different. "I don't know" is a definite conclusion after which there is nothing else. I don't know — full stop.

If you really want to come to terms with reality, you need to be able to accept this "I don't know." What's worse is that there are infinitely more aspects of this life that you can never comprehend than there are aspects you *can* comprehend. You know your name, you know your phone number, you know your shoe size. If you're really clever you might even know your ass from a hole in the ground. You extrapolate from the fact that you know these things and believe that if you got really, really, really clever you might even-tually be able to understand what your life is in the very same way.

---

* Sorry, Richard Gere. Sorry, Mr. Dalai Lama.

You think you might be able to work out the Ultimate Answer and then file it away in your head the way you file away your husband's middle name or your sister's birthday. But you can't do it. No one can. No one. Anyone who tells you otherwise is a lying sack of shit.

Life and death can be explained in various ways. Some of these may be better than others. The idea that people die and then God sends their souls to heaven or to hell is clearly ridiculous. I figured that out by the time I was five, and I have no patience with anyone older than that who hasn't managed to work at least that much out for themselves. Am I making light of some people's very heartfelt religious convictions? Yes. I am. Deal with it.

The idea of reincarnation seems a bit better. At least it gives God more than two options.* But it's still pretty idiotic when you probe it a little further. The reincarnation theories I've looked at always end up with the person getting so pure after like a zillion reincarnations that they end up in some modified version of heaven, so it's not a very good substitute for ideas about dying and getting sent to heaven or hell. Sometimes Zen teachers like to explain life and death with metaphors about rivers and candles. Sometimes they'll say it's like using a lit candle to light another candle, then blowing out the first one. The new flame isn't really the same flame as the old one, but it's not really completely different either. Another explanation has it that our lives are like bubbles on the surface of the river. When those bubbles pop, their existence as bubbles is over once and for all. Yet they were really just expressions of the river, and the river still flows. But even these explanations are still more like words of comfort than anything else.

You won't understand life and death until you're ready to set aside any hope of understanding life and death and just live your life until you die.

---

* Or three, if you're Catholic.

# CHAPTER 10

# *WORKING FOR WEIRD PEOPLE*

*I* had put my work troubles on the back burner while I dealt with my mom's death. But now I was going to have to face them again.

Before I moved to Los Angeles I'd had a long conversation with Tomoyuki Nakano, who was then the president of Nakano Productions but was not anymore, about how the whole thing was supposed to work. One of my stipulations was that I would be able to return to Japan at least four times a year. Mr. Nakano readily agreed. In fact, he said I would be allowed unlimited business trips to Tokyo, plus once every three months I could take a private trip to Japan that the company would pay for.

When Tomoyuki was fired — or quit, depending on whom you ask — three months after I got to LA, all those promises went right out the window. Still, I expected that I'd be going back to Tokyo at least every three months for meetings with my bosses, updates, and instructions. There's only so much that can be communicated through email and telephone.

I'd normally have gone back for my quarterly meeting with them in December or January. But Mom's condition had prevented that from happening. By the end of January, though, I was back at work. Sort of.

Let me explain. When I was first sent out to Los Angeles in late 2004, Nakano Productions had a definite, if somewhat vaguely defined, goal for its US operations. The company would celebrate the thirty-fifth anniversary of their most successful character, Zone Robo, in 2006. The goal was to get some kind of Zone Robo–related production underway in America before the year's end. Maybe it'd be a movie, maybe a TV series, maybe a cartoon. But whatever form it would take, some kind of Zone Robo *something* needed to happen in the US. Even if that something wasn't finished that year, the PR surrounding the start of production could still be used to bolster the character's somewhat flagging — but always impressive — sales figures back in Japan.

Though Tomoyuki's goal was never crystal clear, at least he had a goal. After he was gone, a revolving-door policy among the company's upper management emerged that left everyone at the decision-making level paralyzed with fear. No one wanted to be the guy who instigated a project that failed and then get fired for it. So as a result no one would instigate any projects at all.

The company was still in business. But the only things getting done were the things that were considered safe. The regular avenues of merchandising were duly exploited. Our international sales guys in Tokyo sold the existing Japanese programs to the same handful of Asian buyers they'd sold to a hundred times in the past, and nobody complained.

The problem for me, though, was that no one had ever really exploited the US market. There were no precedents for what I needed to do. Consequently, none of the many suggestions I sent back to the home office ever got the green light or even the yellow light. They were forever "under consideration." As far as I knew the detailed reports I was writing each week were being filed into giant three-ring binders and hidden in a cabinet somewhere. There was no evidence that any of them was being taken seriously.

This had been making me crazy for several months before my mom had died. Sure, my practice had helped me accept it to a certain degree. But it didn't fix the problem. It seemed like every new approach I tried failed. Something needed to be done.

What's more, this work stuff wasn't just frustrating to me. Ever since I'd moved to America I'd been enlisting Yuka's help to rewrite my weekly reports to the company. My Japanese is good enough to be understood. But it's not really professional level. So she would take my mutant sentence structure and ghastly grammar and turn them into presentable, businesslike Japanese. Though she did this for free, there was a price to pay.

Up till then Yuka had listened to my bitching and moaning about the company. But she'd never really been involved with them directly. Now she could see me reporting tremendous opportunities to them week after week and watch as they all got shot down arbitrarily with only the vaguest of reasons. Each time she had to fix up one of these reports she just got angrier, both with Nakano Productions and with me. Why did I stay with such a company full of incompetents?

Well, why *did* I? Honestly I'm not really certain myself. But one of the great practical advantages of the job was that their constant state of indecision left me with a tremendous amount of free time that I could use to promote my books. A couple of times I went to job interviews trying to see what else might be available in Hollywood for a Japanese-speaking person with over a decade of experience in the Japanese film industry. There was no shortage of work. But it was clear that most of the other available jobs would require me to be on duty forty or more hours a week, which would leave very little time to do the stuff I needed to do to keep my career as an author going.*

I also felt like there was some kind of strange connection between me and the Nakano family. I don't want to get all weird and spooky on you, but there was something not entirely rationally explainable about how I'd managed to get my job there and why they kept hanging on to me. I once spoke to Nishijima about this. I told him it seemed like the universe was supporting my Zen teaching through Nakano Productions. I expected him to tell me I was full of shit. But he agreed, saying he felt that way about the job he held for many years at the Ida Cosmetics company.

More than just that, though, I knew I could do this job. I knew I could make Zone Robo a big success in America if they'd just let me do some of the things I kept suggesting. Yes, this is one of those "if only" situations that Buddhist philosophy warns us not to get too involved in. But I was so close with some of these deals I brought to them, that all it would have taken was a signature from Tokyo, and we'd be in business. Quitting my job wasn't a viable option in my opinion.

About a month after my mom died I started suggesting to the company that I ought to make a trip to Tokyo to check in and, more important, to straighten out exactly what I could do to earn the money they were sending me each month.

They refused to have me come out for a meeting. I was completely taken aback by this. Were they actually telling me *not* to come to the home office when my reason for coming was to receive clear instructions about what I was supposed to be doing in America? In other words, were they actually telling me to just sit tight and do nothing while I continued to collect a paycheck? In fact, that's exactly what they were telling me.

---

* Just a little aside here to all you aspiring writers out there — if you find a day job that offers you a flexible schedule, don't quit it. Not only do most publishers pay their authors lousy, they expect you to be able to spend a lot of time running around the country promoting your book, largely at your own expense.

I was getting paid basically to just hang out in Los Angeles. I guess this is what lots of people would call a dream job. Well maybe that's *your* dream job, but it's not mine. I wanted to work. I was not happy being told to sit tight.

Besides that, I was sitting on top of what I knew to be a gold mine for the company. A hotshot young producer at one of the major Hollywood studios — let's call him Mr. Hotshot and the people he worked for Major Hollywood Studios rather than mentioning their actual names — wanted to make Zone Robo into a massive summer blockbuster movie. He envisioned it as what they call a "tent pole film." This means a huge, huge movie with an outrageous budget, big-time stars, and a publicity campaign that would ensure everyone in the country knew who Zone Robo was.

Astoundingly, I could not get the Tokyo offices interested in pursuing this. The only guy who was into it was Mr. Serizawa, who'd recently left his position at a big-deal Japanese film production company's LA offices to work for Nakano in Tokyo. But he couldn't get anyone else there to back him up. I was baffled. What reason would anyone in their right mind have not to follow through on such an offer? The answer was clear. The people at Nakano Productions were no longer in their right minds, if, in fact, they ever had been.

Finally, though, after much begging and pleading I was able to schedule a meeting to talk about this. In May. Eight months since I had last been to Japan. I was very curious to see just what the hell was going on over there.

# CHAPTER 11

# GOAL/NO GOAL

For part of my visit to Tokyo to straighten things out with Nakano Productions I arranged to stay at Nishijima Sensei's itty-bitty apartment in a gigantic government-subsidized apartment complex called Takashimadaira. That's way too long a word to pronounce, so I'll use the name as infrequently as possible.

It's one of the largest housing projects in the world, with endless identical buildings stretching on as far as the eye can see. The project has three train stations pretty much to itself, plus its own supermarkets, restaurants, retail shops, and bars. These places aren't particularly spiffy, but they're not bad. In fact, the project itself is a fairly pleasant place, except for the fact that all the buildings look exactly alike. It's nicely kept up, there's very little litter and almost no graffiti, and the playgrounds between the buildings are actually safe for kids to play in.

When I first met Nishijima he was living in a reconverted company dorm belonging to the cosmetics company he worked for. The president of the company was a big fan of Zen and required all employees to attend Nishijima's three-day zazen retreats at least once every two years. He had lent Nishijima the building to use as a Zen dojo some years before. Until his wife's death Nishijima spent three days a week at his home in a Tokyo suburb and the rest at his dojo. After his wife died he moved into the Zen center full-time.

Nishijima's family viewed his fascination with Zen as something of an eccentricity, one they tolerated but did not much care for. He tried not to burden his wife and daughter with his Zen-related work too much. But he was not about to stop it either.

When the president of the cosmetics company died, his heirs decided they were wasting too much money on useless extravagances like Zen dojos and Zen retreats, and Nishijima found himself abruptly cast out of his longtime home. He took the move in stride, though, and never complained, seeing it as a natural progression in his life and work. From now on, he said, he would devote himself to teaching Buddhism to the whole world "through the method of blog." One of his students had set one up for him, and he was amazed at his new ability to communicate instantly to the entire planet just by typing on his computer keyboard. For someone born in 1919, it must have seemed unimaginable.

While I was at Nishijima's place, I told him about what had been going on with Nakano Productions. I said that they had absolutely no goal for their international business. "In Zen it's important to have no goal," he said. "But in business a goal is absolutely necessary."

When I tell this story people often have difficulty accepting its apparent dichotomy. How can a Zen teacher, dedicated to a goalless practice, function in the business world where goals are essential? But this is only a problem if you're too caught up in words and images and too insistent on maintaining the fiction that all aspects of life must be consistent.

Of course it's important not to be a hypocrite. But there's nothing hypocritical about practicing goallessness in Zen and making specific, goal-oriented plans when you're in a business meeting. Here's how it works. In terms of the Zen view of the true nature of time, the idea of having a goal breaks down into absurdity. There is only the eternal now, so when would you realize your goal?

But human business affairs take place in a different realm. This realm is essentially an artificial construct of the human mind. As human beings we need to interact with other humans. We provide ourselves with means of support from the wider human community by engaging in such useful fictions together.

Even though, in Buddhist terms, there is no real future, I still have a retirement fund. When I go out for public appearances I plan ahead — not very well, mind you — but I do. I need to know where I'm going, how long it will take to get there, how long I'm supposed to speak, and what Thai restaurants in the area will be open when I'm done. You can't function in society if you don't involve yourself in the fictions society accepts about time. But you do so with the understanding that you're playing a game.

A lot of people imagine it'd be wonderful to escape from their everyday lives and run off to some kind of spiritual world where everything is okeydokey and they never have to worry about jobs and all the attendant hassles. This is how cults work, by promising a life free from trouble in exchange for believing stupid stuff and blindly obeying the master. But the truth is that there's no cult, no church, no monastery in the world that is any less susceptible to politics and basic human bull crap than any company or other organization. The dreams we all have of there being some ideal place where we could escape from all such troubles are all just empty fantasies. I dreamed this dream myself for a very long time and still find myself lapsing into it. But it ain't gonna happen. Not to me. Not to you. Not to anyone anywhere in the world at any time.

In Los Angeles people are always hopping from job to job trying to find something better. The culture in SoCal gives the message that as soon as things get rough you run away. And, of course, there *are* times when you have to split an uncool scene* — battering husbands, Bobbitting wives, and that sort of thing are good examples. But if you do split, just make sure you don't do it with the expectation that everything's gonna get solved once and for all.

Our day-to-day real human struggles are important. I hate 'em just as much as anyone else. I especially hated them on this trip since I was going to have to spend the rest of the week trying to explain what I wanted to people who didn't seem to be very interested in understanding. But it's what I had to do. And even if I ran away from this particular struggle now, it would come back and bite me in the ass in another form later on. I wish it wasn't this way as much as you do. But facts are facts. Watch your own life closely, and you'll see it's just the same. You can *always* improve your situation. But you do so by facing it, not by running away. The brilliant thing is that doing what you do is how you realize your life and realize the universe. Your struggles are your true self. Weird, huh?

In any case, Nishijima's take on my troubles at Nakano Productions was that they probably hoped I would take the kind of decisive action they were unable to take themselves. He said they placed those barriers in front of me expecting me to break them. This was so that they could absolve themselves of responsibility, should whatever I do turn out badly. Naturally, should my actions turn out well they would be all too eager to take credit.

He also said that he thought I probably didn't really need them anymore. He believed my own creative works would be able to see me through financially. If he believed that, he obviously hadn't seen the pitiful advances I'd been receiving for my books! A book that took me a year and a half to write would pay my rent in Los Angeles for about six months, maybe eight, if I could forgo eating.

---

* Dig the groovy hippie talk, man.

"Make your own job," he said. "And if it is successful, that is good. If it is not, you can resign."

With that advice in mind I steeled myself to have it out with my bosses.

## CHAPTER 12

# MEETING THREE GODZILLAS
# IN TOKYO

*T*he following day I set off for my scheduled encounter with
my two bosses: Akiyama, the head of my department, a year
younger than me and a dedicated bodybuilder who'd actually won a
couple of citywide competitions, and Miyagi, his boss, an older and
more typical Japanese "salaryman." Here's why I had two bosses.

Japanese companies have an internal ranking system that is used
by nearly every business in the country. In the same way as a corporal in the navy has roughly the same authority and duties as a corporal in the army or a corporal in the marines, a *bucho* (section chief)
in Toshiba Electronics has roughly the same authority and duties as
a *bucho* in Toyota or a *bucho* in Nakano Productions. Thus, when you
get a Japanese person's business card you immediately know pretty
much what level of the company you're dealing with. This is utterly
unlike the film business in the United States, where everyone is a vice
president and no one has any idea what they do, including the vice
presidents themselves.

According to his rank in the company, Akiyama should have

been the decision maker in my department. But he absolutely refused to take responsibility for anything, ever. He always deferred to his superior, who was Miyagi. Unfortunately, Miyagi was also absolutely averse to taking responsibility for anything, ever.

My meeting with Akiyama and Miyagi was long and painful and consisted mainly of me saying stuff they didn't understand and them responding by saying stuff I didn't understand back. Language and cultural barriers were a factor, of course. Japanese is not my first language and, though Akiyama speaks pretty good English, it's not his first language either. Miyagi is one of those guys who likes to tell people he speaks English, though he really doesn't. I lived in Japan for eleven years and understand the language and culture probably about as well as any foreigner can. What was going on here went light-years beyond mere differences in language and business style.

Decades of infighting among the Nakano clan had left the company management devastated and utterly incapable of action. Guys like Akiyama and Miyagi clung tenuously to their jobs by desperately avoiding doing anything the least bit innovative. As long as they kept following established patterns, no one would blame them if things went badly, since they hadn't personally come up with the idea to do whatever it was they were doing.

This worked especially well when you did something that was originally done by a now-deceased* member of the Nakano family. To say you were following one of their plans was practically like saying to a committed Christian that you were following the Bible. The trouble with doing that was much the same as the trouble with following the Bible. Rules and patterns set down in the past were created to deal with the circumstances of their time. They don't always work well in the present. This is especially true in the film business, where the rules change almost by the second. The other trouble in

---

* Or at least considered to be deceased.

our specific case was that most of those established patterns had never really worked very well in the first place. The only advantage they had was that they'd been established by people who were now dead and thus beyond reproach.

I was now proposing that we deal with that producer I'd met in Hollywood to make a big-budget Zone Robo movie. This did not fall into any of the accepted patterns. For either Akiyama or Miyagi to okay such an action would be a leap into the unknown. I understood that. But I still felt like I might be able to convince them by presenting my arguments rationally and citing real stories of how other movies had gone into production the same way and had gone on to make heaps of moola. But nothing I said or did was going to have any effect at all.

Along with the movie proposal I was also suggesting that we participate in an American documentary being shot in Tokyo all about the Japanese special-effects industry. This, I thought, was a no-brainer. I'd sent a number of emails about it that either went unanswered or prompted noncommittal but somewhat positive responses. So I thought we were all set. But I found to my dismay that Akiyama and Miyagi didn't want to do this documentary.

The reason had something to do with the fact that the now-deposed ex-president of Nakano Productions — the man who'd sent me over to Los Angeles to begin with — was also participating in the documentary. I couldn't see why this mattered. Any publicity was good publicity, I thought. We had virtually no brand recognition in America, and this was poised as a well-placed program. It wasn't just good business to be part of this documentary, it was a business necessity.

I made my case, but my bosses wouldn't budge. In the end it was decided we would participate in a very tangential way in the film. But I was forbidden to go to any of the shootings.

Zen practice can help you deal with disappointment by showing you that all of life is characterized by disappointment. Nothing ever lives up to your expectations, no matter what your expectations are. This doesn't mean you're never disappointed. I know I sure was. But you know that disappointment is just the action of your brain re-adjusting itself to reality after discovering things are not the way you thought they were. The best course of action when encountering dis-appointment is to know you now understand the situation better than you did before when all you had to go on was your thoughts. There's no sense wallowing in sadness that you were mistaken. You are for-tunate, in fact, because you're now better equipped to move forward realistically. So that's what I did.

My solution was that I would not follow their order not to attend the shooting. How were they gonna know, anyway? At this point being fired would have been a blessing, so I really didn't care if they did that. It was a good decision because I got to meet three Godzil-las at the same time.

My friend Norman England, who was directing the documen-tary, was conducting interviews at a place called Monsters, the work-shop of Shinichi Wakasa, the guy who built the monster costumes for several of the recent Godzilla movies. Wakasa and I have been friends for a few years, so I got invited to come see his interview. When I arrived I was pretty shocked to see Haruo Nakajima, who played Godzilla from the first movie in 1954 up till 1972's *Godzilla on Monster Island*; Kenpachiro Satsuma, who played Godzilla in most of the '90s films; and Tsutomu Kitagawa, who played Godzilla from the turn of the century until the supposedly final G-film, *Godzilla Final Wars* in 2005, all sitting around a table in back smoking and chatting. I was in shock and awe.

This was the first time all three men had ever been interviewed at the same time. I've been a fan of Godzilla movies since I was a wee lad, so it was unbelievably cool to get to be a part of this historic meeting. I got my photo taken with the three of them and scored some autographs. I was amazed that Nakajima actually recalled meeting me years before. He's pretty old and must meet a lot of fans, including foreign Godzilla-geeks like me. It was a remarkable day.

My goal had been figuring out what was up with Nakano Productions, and I had utterly failed to do so. But something much better happened instead. Things do sometimes work out for the best. But I still had no clue what I was going to do.

## CHAPTER 13

# WORKING FOR THE SUICIDE GIRLS

**M**y dream of making Zone Robo a success in America was dead and buried. I returned to Los Angeles still employed as the American liaison for Nakano Productions. But with even the vague goals I'd started off with pulled out from under me, I had no clue what I was supposed to be doing. The trip I thought would sort things out had just made things more confused and aimless.

Not being the kind of person who can feel good about doing nothing and getting paid for it, I tried to find some strategy that would fit their criterion of being absolutely safe and yet would still help us establish a foothold in the US market. But you can't establish an unknown character in a new market without taking some risks. And so I ended up just sending reports every week that essentially said nothing at all. Nobody complained.

Meanwhile, though, some other stuff had been brewing. Sometime before the trip to Japan I got an email from someone who identified herself as Helen Suicide — though her real name was Helen Jupiter.* Helen ran the newswire section of Suicide Girls — a website

---

\* Honest to Buddha, folks, that's her real last name.

featuring erotic photos of naked punk-rock, emo, goth, and whatever-other-categories-of-alternative-are-out-there girls, often with copious tattoos, multiple piercings, big green Mohawks, or shaved heads. Definitely not *Playboy*!

They also have a newswire service. The word *news* is used here very loosely. It's more like the *Onion* or *MAD* magazine than CNN. As part of the newswire they have several columnists who contribute regular op-ed pieces, including Wil Wheaton* and gonzo comedian Rob Corddry. Helen liked my books and wanted me to be one of their columnists.

There are a whole lot of people out there for whom the word *Buddhism* is just a cover for the same old straitlaced neo-Puritanism beloved by every other religion in the world. They want their Buddhism as clean-cut and shiny as any Southern preacherman who rants about purity from the pulpit while he fucks his lady parishioners on the side. Anything that'll get those guys' knickers in a twist is a worthwhile enterprise, as far as I'm concerned. They need it so desperately. I immediately accepted Helen's offer.

After I'd already said yes, I started to wonder what Nishijima might think of it. After all, I was his dharma heir, and this was a pretty bold step I'd be taking. I thought I'd better get his opinion on it at least. I wasn't exactly looking for his permission. Ours was not the kind of relationship in which I ever felt I needed his okay to do anything.

Still, I thought that if he really hated the idea I might reconsider. So I sent him an email about it with a link to the Suicide Girls page. I even gave him the password they'd given me so he could get the full experience and not just see the more demure photos they put up on their publicly accessible pages. He wrote back right away saying he thought it was a wonderful idea. He said we needed to embrace these kinds of new forms of communication for the spread of Buddhism. He said that he didn't judge art in terms of religious views about

---

\* *Star Trek's* Wesley Crusher.

what was pure and what wasn't. He only judged it in terms of whether or not the images were beautiful. He thought the photos were beautiful.

I shouldn't have worried about what he'd say anyway. Years ago I asked him if he felt there was any dichotomy between his work as a Buddhist teacher and his then-current day job working at a cosmetics company. He said he thought that anything that made women more beautiful helped make the world a more pleasant place. He saw no problem with what his company did.

I'd been doing the Suicide Girls columns for a few months by the time I met Nishijima in Tokyo on my visit to go argue with Nakano Productions. He'd read most of them, and his opinion of them was higher than mine. But I'm a pretty harsh critic of my own writing. I'm sure I'll hate this book by the time you're reading it.

However, Nishijima had a bomb to drop on me when I was visiting him. Years ago he'd started an organization he called Dogen Sangha International. This was a loose affiliation of his own direct students, the teachers he'd ordained, and the students of those teachers. Beyond that, though, no one really knew just exactly what or who Dogen Sangha International was. There was no board of directors or list of members or even a clear definition of what it took to join the group. There was no organization charter or statement of purpose.

At age eighty-eight, Nishijima was becoming more and more aware of his mortality. A broken tailbone had landed him in the hospital for a couple of weeks the previous year, and a subsequent diagnosis of mild diabetes had reminded him just how frail his body was getting. He decided it was time to name his official successor as leader of Dogen Sangha International — whatever it was — and he'd decided on me.

Now, although it's a Buddhist group, Dogen Sangha International was not the most tranquil organization. In fact, some of its members could be downright mean to each other. One of Nishijima's students, I'll call him Zeppo, saw himself as *the* founding member of the organization. Other members had been around Nishijima much longer than I had.* I knew that if I accepted, the moment the old man chose to make his announcement I would instantly become a target.

I'm pretty sure some of these guys already saw me as jockeying for what they considered to be their position as the old man's successor. At least they acted like they did. This would only serve to confirm what they felt they knew all along, that I was some kind of sycophantic interloper who was lobbying for control of the organization. But with God as my witness I swear I wasn't. I hate religious organizations. I had no desire even to join one, let alone lead one. Especially this one, where it would be up to me to define exactly what it was to an already existing membership who I knew would resent me even before I had made my first move.

Still, Nishijima clearly wanted me to do it. This wasn't an arbitrary decision arrived at in a hurry. He'd spent a lot of time working it out. For reasons I'm sure I'll never fully comprehend, he considered me somehow uniquely qualified to take up what he'd started and continue it after he was gone.

But what was it I was supposed to lead, and how? The only thing that was clear was that he expected me to make that clear. He trusted my judgment. Again, I don't even want to speculate about why. He told me he felt I understood the Buddhist philosophy completely and that I was the one who most fully grasped what he'd been trying to say all these years. Huh? Me?**

I told him I'd think about it. I already get enough hate mail from people who don't think I live up to their notions of what a Buddhist teacher should be. Was I really up for even more abuse?

---

\* But only a few of them had been around Buddhism as long as I had. Since they hadn't known me when I'd studied with Tim, though, even guys who'd been studying Buddhism for far fewer years than me tended to see me as a newbie.

\*\* Seriously. This is what he told me and, honestly, I still really don't understand why.

But although I hadn't given him my decision, I knew when I left that I had no choice but to accept. If I said no, who would he ask? He wasn't about to ask Zeppo, no matter what he thought. There was another student of his I'll call Gummo who had a pretty spiffy organization of his own going (more on him later). But I knew the old man didn't really trust him with Dogen Sangha International either. There were only two other guys he could really ask. But they were fairly nice, unassuming people. They might say yes to the appointment. But they wouldn't be prepared for the shit storm that would come as soon as they did. I couldn't do that to them.

So I hemmed and hawed over the matter for a couple of months and finally decided that, as much as I didn't want to do it, it made some kind of sense for me to head this very disorganized organization. So I called Nishijima up one day and said, "Let's do this thing."

## CHAPTER 14

# *THE PORNO BUDDHIST*

*T*he shit storm began almost the minute Nishijima made his announcement. Since he was into spreading Buddhism around the world "using the method of blog," he made the announcement on his blog. That fact alone really pissed off several of his longtime students. But what else was he supposed to do? Send them all a letter? Invite them all to a big get-together in Tokyo? The blog was a perfectly sensible twenty-first-century solution to the problem.

Zeppo promptly sent me a massive email from his dojo in Adelaide, Australia, implying that Nishijima Sensei had become too old and senile to make such a decision on any rational basis. Didn't I understand, he asked, that when people get old they make strange decisions while seeming to be perfectly lucid at other times? He saw Nishijima's decision to appoint me head of the group, I assume, as one of those strange decisions. He asked if I thought "the old man" was somehow cosmically infallible and if I believed this mystical ability would somehow be passed on to me. He went on to hurl some insults about a TV appearance of mine he'd seen on YouTube, saying how ridiculous I looked in my "splendid golden robes waving my stick around." I'd worn my Sunday best Buddhist robes as a concession to my publisher, who thought I'd look cooler on TV that way. Part of the outfit is a little stick you hold for ceremonies. Being nervous, I'd started gesturing with it and was pretty mortified when I saw the video. Zeppo concluded by saying I should "open my eyes" and, I presume, see that he was right, that Nishijima was demented and that I was supremely unqualified to lead our group.

With that vote of confidence, I was off and running. Soon I also became aware that I was apparently known throughout the Buddhist communities of the West as the "Porno Buddhist." This, it seems, was a source of great humor as well since, I was told, these Buddhists enjoy laughing at me because of it. One of Nishijima's students told him this privately, and he told me. That student warned him he was making a grave mistake appointing someone like me to run his organization. I wondered, was it Zeppo again?

In fact it was Gummo, a tall bandy-legged former Christian Scientist and dharma heir of Nishijima's who hailed from Western Canada. A very straightlaced guy, Gummo believed that my association with pornography as well as my well-known "potty mouth" would undermine all of Nishijima's — and by extension Gummo's — good work.

In an email sent to me and copied to all Nishijima's ordained students, Gummo said I was an embarrassment to myself, our teacher, and the entire sangha, and that he would use every resource at his command to turn me into the laughingstock of the Buddhist world. He said I might be able to swindle the sycophantic fanboys who slobber over my every sacred statement* but that he couldn't be fooled. He said I could hide behind my phony baloney hard-assed punk persona, but he would tell the world that I really was "just a clown." He

---

* That means you people reading this, I guess.

finished by saying he would call the temple in Japan where we hold our annual Zen retreats and do everything in his power to get them to cancel this year's retreat.* Another strong show of support.

Now, I don't want to present myself as poor little innocent Brad just minding his own business, with everybody getting mad at me for no reason. I knew when I chose to write for Suicide Girls that this kind of stuff was going to come up. But I did not expect anything quite this vicious from people who used to present themselves as my friends.

I'm not prone to weeping bitter tears over such things. But I was genuinely hurt. I had hoped for some support from my teacher's fellow students. Were the situation reversed, I would never in a million, zillion, quintillion years even have entertained the thought of trying to undermine their position. If I'd really objected to it, the worst I'd have done would be to leave the group. I could not comprehend their behavior at all.

Every time I've pointed out any of this stuff, somebody claims I'm trying to make like I'm the hero and guys like Zeppo and Gummo are the villains. But I think I've already given a pretty clear accounting of my own stupidity and mistakes. If you haven't had enough yet, read on. Oh, I'm a fuckin' hero all right. All shiny and pure, just like John Wayne.** As for Zeppo and Gummo, they have their own lives and their own pain. It's not my wish to add to anyone's misery, which is why I've gone to great lengths to tell the story as accurately as possible without specifying who was actually involved. They're not evil people. But they did say these things, and it did hurt.

Be that as it may, calling me the Porno Buddhist was an interesting line of attack. When this accusation was made, my teacher

---

* He was apparently unsuccessful in convincing them and the retreat went ahead as planned. See chapter 28.
** This is sarcasm. But you knew that.

recommended that my "friends" study a chapter in Dogen's *Shobogenzo* called "Flowers in Space." It's like the old *Muppet Show* skit "Pigs in Space," only with flowers instead of pigs. He said it related well to the Buddhist attitude toward regulating sexual desire.

I won't try and get into the whole chapter in this dime-store novel. You can go buy volume three of Nishijima's translation of *Shobogenzo* if you want to read it all. I'm sure other translations are available as well. I'll just quote you part of it here.

Dogen refers to an old Chinese Zen master who said, "By eliminating disturbances we redouble the disease." Dogen explains this by saying, "We have not been free of disease hitherto; we have had the Buddha bug and the patriarch bug. [The act of] intellectually excluding [that which we do not like] now adds to the disease and augments the disease. The very moment itself of *eliminating* is inevitably *disturbance*. They are simultaneous and are beyond simultaneousness. Disturbances always include the fact of [trying to] eliminate them."

We all have sexual desire. There's nothing particularly wrong with that. We need to have sexual desire to survive as a species. Neither Dogen nor Buddha himself would even have been born were it not for their parents' sexual desire. If you want to believe *your* savior was born without someone having had sex first that's your business.[*] Anyway, the line above doesn't even specifically relate to sexual desire but to the concept of disturbance.

Lots of spiritual-type people try to establish some kind of

---

[*] And, by the way, not even Buddhists are immune to that particular fantasy. There are virgin birth legends about Buddha. Supposedly a white elephant entered his mother's side and a little while later baby Buddha popped out, took seven steps and declared himself to be the coolest guy ever. But these stories were never taken as particularly important. It was never believed that, should it turn out Buddha's dad and mom really did do the nasty it meant that the entire philosophy could be wrong. This is because the veracity of Buddha's philosophy was never viewed as being dependent upon his being divine. These days most Buddhists regard those legends as quaint anachronisms rather than as literal truths to be defended. No offense intended. I'm just sayin'....

spiritual-type purity in their lives. In order to do so they often try as hard as they can to eliminate anything that might disturb that purity. But Dogen says that "excluding adds to the disease and augments the disease." Furthermore, he says that "the very moment itself of eliminating is inevitably disturbance." There is only one reason we call something a disturbance: because we wish it wasn't there. "Disturbances always include the fact of trying to eliminate them." Ain't it the truth!

This is the real key to understanding the Buddhist way. Our practice seeks to expose everything — sort of the way I'm exposing the troubles in my own sangha right here.* It may look like we're doing nothing when we sit zazen. But actually we are exposing ourselves to ourselves. Lots of us who do this don't like what we see. I don't like what I see a whole bunch of the time. Yet we persevere until no rock is unturned and every squishy little bug underneath has seen the light of day.

Perhaps human civilization only really began to advance once sex and nudity became hidden. In the animal world, exposure of the genitals to another member of the same species has only two meanings. One is an invitation to sex, and the other is as a way of inciting combat. Our own species, with its upright posture, has its genitals constantly exposed and must have been continuously sending out fight and/or fuck signals. Maybe it wasn't till we toned that down by covering up that we could get on to other things.

But that was a long, long time ago. In our contemporary world no one can hope to avoid being bombarded by images of objects of desire. In some countries women are forced to cover themselves from head to toe, lest they incite impure desires among men. But if everything that might incite desire should be covered, then oil magnates ought to cover their Cadillacs in big ol' burlap sacks as well. In any

---

* And if you think that other sanghas don't have similar stuff going on, go ahead and think that.

case, we don't live in that kind of society.* For anyone who has an Internet connection, images of sexual desire are available twenty-four hours a day at the touch of a button. Magic!

Y'know, when I think of the incredible trials and tribulations we had to go through when I was a kid just to get a couple of pictures of a naked lady in someone's dog-eared and stained copy of *Penthouse* with the good pages all stuck together. . . . You kids today have it pretty easy. And I actually think this will ultimately make the world a better place, though we may have to go through some rough adjustments first. We need to learn how to live in a world where such things are exposed to public view. And humanity hasn't had to do that for a very long time.

How *do* we live in such a world? How do we conduct ourselves as members of an advanced civilization — built partly by the ancient practice of hiding sex — wherein sex has been put on view to anyone who wants to see it at any time of the day or night? This is a vital question. But like all the most vital questions, it's not one that I or anybody else can answer for you. You have to discover your own way. The only thing I can offer is the advice that you have to constantly seek balance.

When things are too exciting, that's a problem. Just because something is exposed to view doesn't mean you have to look at it. Just because some experience is available doesn't mean you need to have it. Nowadays, though, we can no longer rely on society to hide these things from us so we don't take in too much. We need to create our own discipline.

Every high has a corresponding low. You don't believe that, I bet. Most of us don't. We think someday we'll find that one special high that lasts forever. I can't stop you from searching for it. But I can say without question that it doesn't exist. It is not in the nature of

---

* Apologies if you happen to live in one of those countries where women must cover up by law, but I doubt that many of you do.

things for such a high to exist. We only notice such a high by its contrast to its corresponding low.

Those who hope for purity and righteousness always try and destroy that which disturbs them. They think the disturbance comes from outside themselves. This is a serious problem. Wars, suicide bombings, and all sorts of other nasty things start from the premise that we can destroy "evil" outside ourselves without dealing with the evil within.

I guess my dharma brothers thought that what disturbed them was located in an apartment in Los Angeles dressed in golden Buddhist robes surrounded by plastic monster toys and dozens of luscious Suicide Girls.* But I have my doubts. Whenever I looked carefully at the things that disturbed me most deeply, I never found them outside me. They were always right here. And that's where they'll always be found.

---

* Oh, how I wish!

## CHAPTER 15

# NO SIN, OR HOW I SPENT
# MY FOURTH OF JULY

**B**ut rather than let Gummo have all the fun exposing me for what I really am, let *me* tell you some scandalous stuff about me. I know all the details way better than he does.

See, Gummo was all about how Brad *might* break the precepts and ruin everything for Dogen Sangha. So let me tell you about some precepts I *have* broken. Among the Buddhist precepts it seems like the hardest one for a lot of people is the one about alcohol and drugs. Depending on which version of the precepts you read, it can be phrased as anything from "Don't live by selling liquor" to "No selling of wine, no drinking of wine" to "No use of intoxicants" and about a dozen or so other variations. I want to tell you the scandalous story of how I broke that one big-time this summer. For those of you who don't know all the precepts, we'll get to the rest of them a bit later. Don't you worry.

Anyhow, I drank alcohol, looked at naked titties, and smoked pot on the Fourth of July, 2007. I'm glad my mom's no longer alive to read that. Not that I'm glad she's dead. Just that I wouldn't want her reading that I smoked pot.* Maybe it doesn't matter anyway, because I wrote about smoking pot and doing acid in my first book, and she was alive when that came out. If she was upset about those parts she never mentioned it.

What I learned from the experience is this — while looking at titties is ultimately no big deal, I should not smoke pot or drink. I can't speak for anyone else. And who cares if I do anyway, because no one needs to listen to me. But I can say with absolute certainty that alcohol and drugs are no good for me. I have strong suspicions they aren't very good for anyone else either. But, like I said, who gives a shit what I think about that?

The situation was this. Greg, a guy who comes to my zazen classes on Saturdays in Santa Monica, invited me to come spend the Fourth at his apartment, where there's a swimming pool. The plan was to waste the entire day lollygagging by the pool. I don't usually like to waste time just doing nothing. But I'd been running around a lot all summer. By July the idea of spending a day in which absolutely nothing would get accomplished sounded very good to me, so I accepted the invitation. I brought along a package of fake hot dogs, some pretzels, and some weird snacks made by Frito-Lay of Japan that were supposed to taste like *gyoza* — what we Americans commonly call "pot stickers." They tasted more like spicy Cheetos. But whatever.

---

* Though I imagine she could deal with the titties and alcohol parts. I know it's good to be truthful, by the way. But there are some things you don't need to shove in your mom's face. Which brings up another good point. While it's vital to be open and honest, it's really not necessary to tell everybody everything all the time. Lots of times what passes for truthfulness is just egotism — "Hey! Lookee me! I did this!" It's hard sometimes to know where to draw the line. If you know that the truth about some incident might hurt someone and that there is no real reason that person needs to know those details, it may be best to keep your mouth shut. As I keep saying, though, nobody can give you any hard-and-fast rule to follow. It's up to you to assess the situation and follow your intuition.

So I get there, and Greg's girlfriend, Teddy,* was making sangria in a big bowl, cutting up apples and oranges and letting them float around inside and dumping sugar into the mess. We took this stuff and our food out to the pool and began our day of lollygagging. Teddy chose not to wear the top half of her bikini. This took me a bit by surprise. But she's got a nice rack, and if she wants to show it to everyone, who am I to object? I guess that's more of the Porno Buddhist in me. I'm sure Gummo would've been duly scandalized. A member of the sangha in a swimming pool with a topless woman? *Oh, the horror!* After about ten minutes the novelty wore off, and it hardly mattered anymore. Though lots of guys from the other apartments kept stopping by our party for some reason.

As the day wore on, everyone was guzzling the sangria. It looked kind of tasty, so I poured myself half a glass. Now, keep in mind that I haven't had so much as a mouthful of alcohol in about ten years or more. I don't have anything against alcohol, really. I just hate the feeling it gives me. I guess that makes me weird. But fine. Everyone else in the whole wide world seems to enjoy being drunk. Yet the few times in my life that I've been drunk, I always hated it.

I've never had much trouble following the Buddhist precept against taking intoxicants because I simply do not like being intoxicated. I've seen the other members of Nishijima's group drinking from time to time. Someone who went out with Nishijima one New Year's Eve said the old man himself had a glass of sake that night. But I know this is not a regular thing for him. As for the people who sit zazen with me now, I don't really get involved. They know what the precepts are, and it's up to them what they do about them.** In Buddhist society as a whole, it seems that the no-intoxicants precept is adhered to most of the time, but drinking in moderation is

---

* Short for Theodora.
** Buddhist teachers who tell their students how to live their lives should be avoided like the plague, if you ask me.

generally acceptable. And "moderation" here would mean like a handful of times a year. Again, it's really up to you.

Anyway, the sangria, I have to admit, was very tasty. I especially liked eating the bits of apple that had been soaking up alcohol for the past several hours. Of course, that's the worst thing for a nondrinker to do, since those little pieces of fruit probably had more alcohol in them than several glasses of the sangria itself. Pretty soon I felt really ill and had a massive headache, which is how alcohol usually affects me, which is why I don't care for it.

Later on after it got dark the group decided to head to another party. This one was on a roof of a seedy apartment building in a dangerous area of Hollywood. The main attraction was that the roof offered a 360-degree view of about a dozen fireworks displays in the area. I was recovering by then. But I was definitely still buzzed. And I didn't much like it. But I like looking at fireworks, so I figured it could be fun.

So we were up there on the roof, and everybody's getting more and more plastered. This roof, by the way, wasn't really designed for hanging out on. There were no protective guardrails or anything like that. It was strictly utilitarian. But there were all kinds of people up there, including a group of gnarly-looking teenagers — the kind I'd have walked down another street to avoid if I saw them hanging out on a corner at night. Our host explained that they were local kids who did not live in the building but they were the ones who'd "discovered" the roof. Meaning they'd found the way to break through the service door and get up there. They liked to go out on the roof and smoke dope. They were generally good-natured, so our host decided it was better to befriend them than to try and chase them away.

So these kids were hanging out with us and passing around joints. At one point I was sitting with a group of them, and the joint came to me. Normally I would have just passed it to the next guy. But I decided it was a good time to experiment. I used to smoke some dope when I was a teenager. I initially gave it up more because it was hard to get hold of than for any deeply philosophical reason. Later on when I got into punk I discovered the philosophy of straight-edge — where you don't drink, do drugs, or have meaningless sex. I went for the first two in a big way. The last one was easy enough to stick to since I was in a hardcore band and our audience was almost entirely guys. I stopped smoking the stuff altogether then.

Still, I always kind of wondered if I'd like it if I did it again. While I'd always hated the effects of alcohol, I used to enjoy marijuana. So I decided to try it and see. I took a big hit, and then a couple more when the joint made the rounds again.

God, I hated it.

Maybe there was a time when I enjoyed feeling dizzy, spaced out, and stupid. But not anymore. I could feel my nervous system becoming unbalanced, and all I wanted to do was to set it right again, but that was impossible because I now had some weird chemicals running around my system. As soon as the buzz started hitting me I wanted it to be over with.

What's worse, though, was that it kept on going for the next two days. Look. I know what some of you are thinking. It's the old bullshit they hand you in school about the effects of THC not wearing off for several days. Well, believe what you want. But I felt like shit for the following day and a good portion of the next. I imagine the only reason I never noticed that pot did this to me when I was younger was because I was so keenly out of tune with my own state of body and mind. If you don't think it works that way for you, you are free to believe that.

This experience had me thinking about what the precept against intoxication really is and why such a precept exists. Folks who like to alter their brain chemistry because they think it reveals subtle layers of the truth argue that our usual state of body and mind is somehow inadequate and that a chemically altered state can open the doors of perception. But I don't think so. All our chemically altered states impair the senses. Try riding a bus driven by someone opening their doors of perception with LSD. Not that I would ever do such a thing. I just wonder why "opening the doors of perception" seems to include the inability to operate a motor vehicle. Shouldn't a true opening of the doors of perception make you a more competent driver? After all, you're supposedly perceiving everything more clearly, right?

I won't deny that drugs can sometimes seem to open up areas of the consciousness we don't normally open and that they can do so very quickly. But they are a very bad way to do this. Whenever you use a drug to achieve some desired effect it's like tuning a piano with a sledgehammer. If your aim is good maybe — *maybe* — you'll get the one string you're aiming at in tune. But you'll wreck the rest in the process. Also, some things should not be done too quickly, and ripping through states of unusual consciousness is one of them.

Our normal state at any given moment, sucky as it may be, is the best and most balanced we can achieve at that moment. Through meditative practice we can gradually improve this state to the point where any level of consciousness available to someone on any kind of hallucinogenic drug becomes available without the use of drugs and without the attendant sensory impairment and collateral damage of drug use.

Something like a drug-induced euphoria is often a part of the meditative experience. But in Zen we try to avoid these states of euphoria or bliss. The reason we avoid them is because they're just as unbalanced as our so-called normal states of mind. Euphoria is the other side of terror. Just because you're only paying attention to one side doesn't mean you're not getting both. True balance of body and mind is very comfortable and pleasant, but it's not euphoric or blissful.

The precept against using intoxicants was laid down by Buddha because he understood the damage drugs can cause. And he understood how the use of drugs impairs our ability to perceive our true condition. But the precepts are not lists of sinful activities.

The weird thing about the precepts is that after you do your practice for a while it becomes effortless to keep them. This happens to everyone to some degree. You simply don't want to abuse your body and brain anymore once you start seeing how nice it feels to keep things in balance. You keep the precepts not because you fear punishment from God or Buddha or you fear being outted by the likes of Gummo and his crew, but because you want to. That's a far more powerful incentive.

I don't know if my experiment was strictly necessary. I mean, I knew I didn't like this stuff before. But I don't regret having done it. Now at least I'm absolutely certain when I say that drugs and alcohol do not interest me.

Titties I still like, though. Sorry, Gummo.

# CHAPTER 16

# *MISUSING SEX*

**W**hile we're on the subject, let's talk about another precept I broke over the summer. It's the precept that's usually given as "Do not misuse sex." Nishijima Sensei's version goes, "Do not desire too much." In either case I broke it. So let me tell you how I, a married Buddhist monk, went out and fucked someone who was not my wife.

Though my job at Nakano Productions was not going well, to say the least, I still had some duties I was expected to perform for them. One of those was going to the FanTasia Film Festival held each July in Montreal. As you can probably guess, the FanTasia Film Festival is dedicated to showing fantastic films from Asia. One of the first films they ever showed back in the mid-nineties was our then-current Zone Robo motion picture. Since then they've shown at least one Zone Robo film at each of their events. In the past decade FanTasia has grown to be one of Canada's biggest film festivals. This year we would once again be presenting the newest Zone Robo adventure.

In past years I'd been extremely enthusiastic about showing our films there, since the major studios were starting to take note of the festival and to send reps there to look for the elusive "next big thing." But the company back in Tokyo had been so unsupportive of my efforts it had begun to feel like a one-man show. This year I was mainly looking forward to hanging out in Montreal rather than entertaining any hopes of the folks at Nakano Productions even taking notice of what I was doing there.

My first day there I got invited to go out with a bunch of festival organizers to entertain a group of Japanese filmmakers who'd come to the event. A couple of the guys there were cutting-edge directors, some of whom had cut their teeth working on Zone Robo movies and TV shows. But I didn't pay a whole lot of attention to them. I was more fixated on Shizuko, the strikingly beautiful niece of one of the guys who was showing his film at the festival. She had gotten roped into acting as an interpreter since she happened to be going to school in Montreal. Born in Shanghai but raised in Hokkaido, Japan, by parents who insisted she learn French, she could speak nearly every language the festival needed interpreters for. She was so cute and friendly and so extremely intelligent I just fell for her the moment we started talking.

By this point Yuka and I hadn't slept together for at least six months. I can't begin to express how sad it was going to sleep every night in our bed while she spent the night by herself out in the living room on a futon. We'd been best friends for so long, and now we hardly even spoke.

The problems had started even before my mom died. She just became more and more distant and withdrawn from me. Much, much later she told me she'd been seeing someone else, though I'm still not sure if that had started before or after she stopped sleeping with me. But at this point I had no idea about that. It just seemed completely random. Also, I was no great shakes as a husband. I was gone all the time, and when I was home I was usually depressed about my job.

Additionally, Yuka has a work ethic that borders on the patho-
logical. I almost never saw her. She left early and came home late
and exhausted. I know she resented the fact that I was getting paid for
doing nothing. She also resented the fact that I was too spineless to
quit, though I'd told her often enough the practical reasons for staying with Nakano Productions since, by this point, they were effectively paying me to promote my books.

We'd talked about our problems some, but nothing ever got
resolved. There was no anger. No drama. It just wasn't working anymore. I was sad about this. I suggested counseling a number of times,
but Yuka refused to go. Nothing I did or said seemed to be able to
break through the rock-hard shell she'd built around herself. At one
point she told me that although she still respected me as a teacher
and a friend, she no longer saw me as a man.

Ouch.

Of course I'd thought some about Leilani, the girl who came to
my Zen classes who I had the big crush on. But she was my student.
Though I never think of the people who come to sit with me as my
students. They're more like "zazen buddies," the way normal people have drinking buddies or golf buddies. In any case, Leilani
hadn't been coming to class for a while, and I'd lost touch with her.
I figured that she was like a lot of people who show up and then disappear. Zazen seems cool for a while, but then they get sick of it, and
I never see them again.

In Montreal I started following Shizuko around like a dog following a meat wagon. I took every chance I could to hang out with
her. I must have looked like a stalker. But she didn't seem to mind.
In fact, she invited me to go with her to see one of her uncle's movies
and accompany her to the party afterward.

As a Zen master I refused, of course. Such temptations must be
avoided.

Ha! You better fucking believe I went. I woulda followed that little piece of tail anywhere. Of course I know that no woman is a mere

"little piece of tail." But every man, and I mean every one of us humans with penises, from His High Holiness Dharma Master Love Peace and Crumbcakes right on down, has times in his life when all the nice spiritual thoughts in his beatific mind fizzle into fluff and the only thing he can fixate on is a nice piece of tail. You may want to believe there are men for whom such urges arise and pass like the clouds floating through a clear blue sky. It never happens that way, I'm afraid. Never. There are, of course, men of great self-control who can resist such temptation and remain calm, cool, and collected. But you'd be surprised how few. It's also somewhat easier to have this kind of self-control if you happen to be really, really old. And when you're in a relationship that's working it's easier to avoid this kind of thing too. I most definitely was not. On the other hand, stories of holy men who've lost their composure in the face of a fine, or even not-so-fine, piece of tail are legion. And, friends, Shizuko was some fine tail. Plus, I genuinely liked her. She was bright and funny and friendly to me in a way no woman had been friendly to me in a long, long time.

I followed her to the movie — which was pretty good, actually — and to the bar afterward for the party with the people involved in the screening. I looked into those big, dark-brown eyes of hers, and I knew that what I wanted most out of life at that moment was to fuck her like a crazed mountain gorilla.* At the same time I was feeling thoroughly unfuckable. If there's a better dick limpener than having your wife say she no longer sees you as a man, then I don't even want to know what it is. But Shizuko seemed like she might be ever so slightly attracted to me, or at least flattered by my obvious attraction to her. Plus, there was a connection there that I can't really explain. She *got* me in ways not many people do, and I got her.

By a very weird coincidence I just happened to have been lent a bicycle by a friend I was staying with in the city who just happened

---

*   Sorry to be so blunt. But that's the honest truth of the matter.

to live not too far from Shizuko. We decided to bike home together. Her place was about ten minutes beyond where I was staying. We were about to go our separate ways. I could have ended it right there and been the hero of this story, the young* Zen master with immense self-control who could sit here telling all of you how you should learn to restrain your sense desires just like me.

But I didn't. Instead I asked her if she'd sit and talk with me a while at a conveniently located bus stop. It was close to 3 a.m. by then. She said yes. I was amazed.

I told her everything. I told her I thought she was beautiful and I wanted to spend as much time with her as I could before I headed back to California. I also told her I was married and that my wife wasn't sleeping with me anymore. I told her I was a so-called Zen master and should not under any circumstances be making such a proposal.

She thought about it for a long time. Finally, she said she'd like me to come back with her to her place. Based on one condition. I'd share her bed. But it would be strictly platonic. She liked me. She even admitted to being attracted to me. But she didn't want a relationship like that and besides, I'd be back in Los Angeles the following day. I agreed. We'd share the bed, but I wouldn't lay a finger on her. And, at the time, I meant it. Seriously.** We got to her room, and she made me turn around as she changed into a big ol' pair of sweatpants and a T-shirt. We crawled into bed and said our goodnights.

I guess I should have realized that nuzzling up against her neck might bring about some kind of a reaction. "*Onegai*," she whispered. That means "please" in Japanese. It's a word I hadn't heard spoken so breathlessly in a very long time. Who am I to refuse such a request? So I continued nuzzling, and pretty soon we were all over each other.

---

\* Young-ish, anyway.
\*\* No, really, I did. I swear.

"Wait," I said, a little breathless. "We said we weren't going to do this."

"I know," she said, kissing me again, harder this time as her hand strayed into the waistline of my pants.

I was genuinely surprised. Here I'd been believing Yuka's assessment that I was thoroughly uninteresting as a sex object, and now this smoking-hot woman was making a grab for my goods. Maybe Yuka had been wrong. . . .

There are a few books out there about Buddhism and sex. Bernard Faure's *The Red Thread* is a good one, and so is *Lust for Enlightenment* by John Stevens. You can read them and learn all about what Buddhists of the past have said about sex, the various doctrines that have been put forward, the ways that sex among monks and nuns has been regulated. You can read about Ikkyu, the Japanese Zen monk who frequented brothels and wrote love poems to a blind prostitute. There are precedents that would condemn what I did and precedents that would exonerate it. There are masters of the past whose behavior makes me look like the world's worst sinner and masters whose behavior makes me look, if not saintly, then at least a little more self-controlled than they were. There are modern Buddhist masters known as much for their drunken orgies as for their enlightened teachings, and there are modern Buddhist masters who are the very models of chastity and virtue.

Nishijima Sensei once told me he thought the monks he ordained should either be married or celibate. Up until that night I'd been both for the better part of a year. But now? Well, I was married. But I guess I hadn't really lived up to his ideals. Still, he'd made it clear this was his recommendation of a way to live a simpler, less troubled life. It wasn't grounds for being disrobed.*

I'm not telling this story to hold up what I did as an example of

---

* Shizuko and I had already disrobed! Har!

"enlightened behavior" that others should imitate. It obviously was not. So don't imitate it. Some people really worry about stuff like that. They think that any time a religious authority figure reveals anything less than an exemplary aspect of his or her life it's an invitation for others to follow suit. But I'm not a religious authority figure, and if you imitate my behavior you do so at your own risk. And, by the way, if you're inclined to believe that other Buddhist teachers don't have sex lives because you've never read about them, go right ahead.

I'm telling this story to report honestly about my life and how my Buddhist practice figured into every aspect of it. There was a difference in how I'd dealt with the situation of being in bed with a highly desirable woman who was not my wife after having done twenty-five years of Zen practice as compared to how I might have dealt with it had I not looked into my own desires and sources of suffering so deeply. And the difference was this: I cannot claim that I was out of control of the situation even for an instant. At the movie theater. At the bus stop. In bed. At each step of the process I was fully aware of every option.

I could have preserved the moral high ground. I could have been the guy who could write a book about how I'd resisted the most irresistible of temptations. I saw the way out at every juncture right up until the deed was done. But I chose to go the other way. Now I would have to accept the results.*

Dogen said that realization does not break the individual any more than the reflection of the sky breaks a dewdrop. Realization also does not make your dick fall off or your pussy shrivel up and go numb. And if you still want to believe that some other more Enlightened Being would never even have thoughts of sex, let alone act on them, I will leave you with your fantasy while I remain with my memories of a very real and special night.

---

\* Or consequences. Same thing.

## CHAPTER 17

# IF YOU'RE GOING TO SAN FRANCISCO BE SURE TO WEAR SOME REALITY IN YOUR HAIR

My trip to the San Francisco Zen Center in summer 2007 started off like this.

Blllllaaaaaaarrrrrnnnnnnggggggghhhhhhhhnnnnnnnnnnnn!!!!!!!!!!

What the fuck? I bolted out of bed in my West Hollywood apartment to the loudest noise I have ever heard in my life. Louder than Zero Defex turned up to eleven thousand. Louder than Godzilla after a busload of triple-garbanzo burritos. Louder than the combined screeches of rage of Zeppo *and* Gummo when they read that last chapter. At first I thought some piece of audio equipment in the house had gone nutso and had started feeding back like crazy. So I'm running all over the place trying to figure out what on God's green earth could make such an obnoxious noise. Out in the living room Yuka was awake too. Not even she could sleep through that, and she sleeps through everything.

Finally we figured out that the noise was coming from outside our apartment as well as inside. When I opened the door I could smell smoke. I could see neighbors on every floor running around trying to figure out what was happening. None of the apartments was spouting flames. I looked at my watch. It was just before five in the morning.

I called 911 on my cell phone, and I got one of those recorded messages like you get when you're calling the DMV or something. "Your call is important to us. Please stay on the line. Calls will be taken in the order they are received." Jesus H. Christ! I could be getting raped by Cossacks or something, and they're putting me on hold? With Muzak too? After a couple of minutes an operator came on, and I told her my building was on fire. She said they were sending the fire guys and that I should wait in the front of the building. Good advice.

Meanwhile, Yuka had also called from our land line and she got through a lot faster. Do they take calls from women in distress before they take them from men?

The fire department finally arrived with two big, shiny fire trucks, all screaming sirens and flashing lights. They stretched the ladder up to the roof of the apartment. Impressive. I kept waiting to see if one of them was gonna race up there. But nobody ever did. Which I felt was a rip-off. Anyway, as it turns out, the fire was in the dumpster in the underground garage. It was already out by then, having been doused by the sprinkler system. But that didn't stop the smoke from setting off the alarm.

I couldn't go back to bed after that. So I did my zazen and my morning yoga, ate some cereal, and got to work doing all the stuff required to keep Nakano Productions paying me. Even though by now I was just treading water.

In spite of all my personal crap, though, I was pretty jazzed about the trip up north. San Francisco is the place where Zen Buddhism really got its start in America. A few books appeared in the early-twentieth century, and the Beat poets liked to say the word *Zen* a lot. But it wasn't until 1959 when Shunryu Suzuki washed up on our shores that Zen as a practice really began to be established here. I mentioned him earlier, but he merits mentioning again in more detail.

The best book about Suzuki's story is *Crooked Cucumber* by David Chadwick. If you want details, read that. Basically, Suzuki was a Zen monk who got sent to the US with the idea that he'd be a minister to the Japanese community living in San Francisco. But then young non-Japanese Americans began turning up at his doorstep wanting to know about this Zen stuff they'd read about in all those Beatnik books. Instead of turning them away, Suzuki decided to teach them.

Pretty soon the San Francisco Zen Center began to grow exponentially. I told you before how he brought over Dainin Katagiri, the guy who established the Clouds in Water Zen Center where I did my talk in St. Paul, and Kobun Chino to be his assistants. Since Kobun was the teacher of my first Zen teacher, Tim McCarthy, I've always felt a connection to the San Francisco Zen Center.

I'd gotten in contact maybe a year before with a guy named Greg Fain,* who was the treasurer there. Greg, an ex–punk rocker who'd once shared an apartment with the drummer of the Dead Kennedys, liked my books so he fixed me up with a speaking gig at the center. I'd finally hit the big time! For me this was like getting a show at Madison Square Garden or Carnegie Hall. How do you get to the San Francisco Zen Center? Do practice, do practice, do practice.

My job was to deliver their weekly after-dinner speech held each Friday. Dinners at the Zen Center are open to the public and consist of delicious vegetarian meals cooked by the residents. That week it was Mexican food. Yum. Silence is observed until the meal verse is chanted, and then everybody gets to talk.

I saved most of my own talking for the speech I gave after everybody got through eating. I don't really remember what I said. But Kim Corbin, the long-suffering publicist who got assigned the task

---

* Greg Fain is not the same Greg whose Fourth of July party I went to, by the way.

of flogging my second book, was there and wrote down the questions I got asked at the end. Here's a couple.*

Q: Will you speak about the different levels of reality, the relative and the absolute?

A: In the strictest terms only this reality we're living in is absolute reality. What we call "relative reality" is just our imagination.

We may think that we're living down here in "relative reality" while all the really important stuff is going on way over there somewhere in "absolute reality." But that's just like imagining that while we're here on earth, which is mundane and boring, somewhere else there's heaven, which is way cool.

The problem for us humans is that we have very big and very clever brains. We use these brains to manipulate images of reality so that we can do incredible stuff like building giant suspension bridges or putting people on the moon or making a really tasty cheesecake. That's all well and good. But the representations of reality we create in our brains are so amazingly lifelike that we get confused and take them for reality itself. For lots of us, the images of reality we create in our heads are far more compelling than reality itself.

It's the reality we create in our brains that we might call "relative reality." It's separate from absolute reality in the sense that it's just an imitation of reality. We don't live there. We can't live there. We live right now, this very minute, only in absolute reality. We don't need to be conscious of absolute reality. The only thing we need to do is to give up the notion that our images of reality are real.

That's easier said than done, though. Nearly everyone we've ever come in contact with has absolute faith in the collective image of reality the human race has built up over a million years. We've

---

* The answers aren't necessarily the same as the ones I gave that day since nobody wrote those down. But they're pretty close, I think.

been taught, from the moment of birth, to ignore actual reality in favor of a very cleverly constructed image of reality.

There's no shortcut to undoing this conditioning. No quick fix. But with continuous practice over a period of years you can let it unravel, and absolute reality will become apparent and clear. Yet you will still retain the ability to deal with the human construct of reality as well.

Q: What is the authentic self?

A: You probably already know that lots of Eastern philosophies have the idea that there is some kind of true self that resides in the body and leaves when the body dies. "I am not this body," they say, "I am the spirit-soul that flies within." But Buddha said this idea was pure nonsense.

Still, the idea of there being an authentic self is not without merit. But the true self is not something personal. It's not *your* self or *my* self. When you were a child you were aware of this universal sense of self. But your parents were confused. They told you it was wrong to believe your self was universal. Rather, they said, this sense of self was something unique to you alone. They didn't do this to be mean or anything. It's the way they'd been taught by their parents, and it's the way their parents had been taught, and so on and on down through countless generations.

In zazen practice you gradually clear away a lot of the ideas you've held for a long time. As you see these ideas one by one as the mistakes they actually are, you progress to more and more deeply held ideas. Once you're ready you may be able to take the leap and accept that even this idea of a personal self, which you feel is the most real thing in all the universe, is also a mistake. Voilà! The authentic self comes shining through.

Q: Is there any relationship between your work as an indie rock musician and your work as a Buddhist monk?

A: The first place I can recall feeling the sense of acting completely intuitively without regard to thought was while playing music on stage. My experiences as a musician were a stepping stone toward what I later experienced more deeply through zazen.

There's something powerful and sacred about silence. So there's obviously a huge difference between zazen and rock music. But any kind of art can communicate something authentic and can be a way to experience real action. So I don't see any necessary conflict between playing rock music and practicing zazen.

I actually saw for myself the relationship between zazen and stuff that's clearly way different from zazen in one of the most un-Zen-like settings you could possibly imagine. Read on.

# CHAPTER 18

# OZZFEST

**I**'m stoned. Did that just happen?" she said, "she" being Melinda, a hanger-on backstage at Ozzfest 2007 in San Bernardino County, California. I told her that indeed "that" had just happened. The "that" in question was that someone had tripped over some bottles behind the stage and made a big noise. Melinda was trying to get close to D. Randall (Randy) Blythe, lead throat shredder of heavy metal megastars Lamb of God — who are *not* a Christian rock band — and she knew I was hanging out with him. She was also simultaneously running away from someone she called "Leatherface." I was unable to determine whether or not this was actually the guy who played Leatherface in the movie *Texas Chainsaw Massacre*. In any case, Melinda seemed to think he was the real Leatherface and told me, "He runs with a chainsaw, and he thinks I'm going to fuck him?"

I assumed the question was rhetorical.

Randy came offstage and apologized for being so stinky. Melinda made sure he knew that I had saved her from Leatherface. He didn't seem much concerned and went back to the band's bus to change clothes. Melinda didn't seem to notice and sorta wandered off. Me and my friends Bret and Ronny just stood there taking it all in.

I never expected teaching Zen to get me backstage at Ozzfest. Randy had invited me because he was a fan of my books. We'd been emailing each other for a few months. He had gotten interested in Buddhism some time ago and picked up my first book shortly after it came out. He first wrote me just before Lamb of God was about to tour Japan, thinking I still lived there and we could meet. But by the time I got his email I was already living in Los Angeles. So after a couple more email exchanges we finally figured out the most convenient place we could see each other was when Ozzfest hit Southern California. Ozzfest, if you don't know, is a big-ass heavy metal festival featuring tons of bands headed up by Ozzy Osbourne, ex–lead singer of Black Sabbath. The festival was plowing its way across America with Lamb of God opening for Ozzy himself.

Ozzy's *Blizzard of Ozz* and *Diary of a Madman* albums were a big deal for me when I was in high school. I even briefly sported a hairdo based on that of Ozzy's firebrand guitarist, the late, great Randy Rhoads. It was a major shock when Rhoads died on March 19, 1982, just fourteen days after my eighteenth birthday. I'd spent countless hours down in my basement figuring out how to play the "classical" bit of the solo to "Flying High Again" and was looking forward to seeing what he'd do next.

I've been backstage at my own fair share of rock-and-roll events. But none of the bands I was in ever had a road crew or a tour bus or a semi for our equipment. And we sure never played anything remotely resembling Ozzfest.

Dogen always cautions against pursuing fame and wealth, as do pretty much all the great Buddhist masters. I used to take that as meaning they thought we should be more austere and have less fun. I assumed that fun was somehow bad in Buddhist terms and they wanted us all to be dour little fuddy-duddies who hated anything enjoyable. I think this misunderstanding of Buddhism is pretty widespread, since lots of people who show up at Buddhist centers seem determined to be the crabbiest wet blankets you'd ever want to meet.* Yet I've never met an actual Buddhist teacher who was the kind of sour stick-in-the-mud some of these guys seem to want to be. Much as history likes to paint Dogen as some kind of dour, funless dude, I tend to doubt that image myself. He was, after all, a guy whose books are full of bad puns and who likened Buddhist teaching to "a whiff of fart or the smell of shit."

It's not anti-Buddhist to have a good time. I've come to a different understanding of why the old masters always cautioned against pursuing wealth and fame. In my work in the entertainment business I've been able to observe a number of rich and famous people at close range, and I've seen how the pursuit of wealth and fame makes them crazy. It's a form of sustained envy and greed. There's always someone richer or more famous than you. There's always another ladder to climb. And it's a 24/7 job either to constantly remind everyone around you that you are a rich and famous person or to try and hide from people who want something from you. It's always really interesting to watch famous people trying to get noticed and then acting all annoyed when it happens. You see a lot of this in LA.

Though he was never wealthy, Dogen himself was pretty famous in his day, so he knew what he was talking about. It's not so much wealth and fame as the mad *pursuit* of wealth and fame for its own sake that he cautions us about. But sometimes an artist does what he or she does, and lo and behold, fame follows. When that happens either you can run and hide, or you can keep on doing what you do. That seems to have been what happened to Dogen and to Lamb of God as well. Lamb of God was a hardworking band whose hard

---

* Not all or even most of them, for sure. But this does seem to be a significant demographic.

work paid off. They never set out to be stars. But now they were, and each member of the band was taking it a little differently. In Randy's case it got him interested in seeking something more real than fame, and he sought that something through Buddhism.

Watching Lamb of God from backstage was a trip. When you're standing where we were you really can't differentiate any of the sounds except the drums. So it all came across like one gigantic roar. But I was able to hear Randy dedicate their song "Redneck" to me. I was honored. But wait! Was he calling me a redneck? The security dudes kept getting more zealous about proving they were doing their duty. They started pushing us farther and farther back from where Randy had told me and my friends to stay.

Later on the crowd was tossing a beach ball around, and it landed onstage. One enormously fat security guy snagged it and proceeded to stab it repeatedly with a sharp object until it died. Poor beach ball. I would have named it Wilson. Every couple of minutes a different security dude would come around with a flashlight and make sure everyone behind the stage had the proper passes and then push us back so we could see and hear even less of the show. A crowd of teenage girls wandered in from somewhere. Were they relatives of someone in the organization? Were they a school trip gone horribly wrong? Were they groupies in training? I'll never know. The security dudes booted them out and tried to send us with them till we showed them our all-access stickers. For, like, the fifth time.

But when they scooted us all the way to the very rear of the stage I was finally able to confirm something I'd always suspected. Those big walls of amps metal bands use? Fake. Not only were they not wired up, they weren't even designed to be wired up. But this is fine. It would look crappy to have the whole band playing through a bunch of lines connected into the public address system, which they actually were.

Randy said there'd be a big-ass backstage barbecue so we should come hungry, which we did. He snagged a Boca burger for me, but the rest of the people there ate nothing but meat. Seriously. These guys didn't even have buns for their bratwurst or chips to go with their buffalo wings. Just piles and piles of meaty meat.

I soon found myself in the midst of a huge gang of drunken hairy guys in biker clothes and drunken women whose only common feature was the giganticness of their breasts, all of them getting more and more plowed on Jägermeister, which sponsored the event, by the minute. I wouldn't have gone within ten feet of the crowd I was in the middle of if I'd been passing by. But here among them I felt pretty safe. Besides, as tough as they looked, even metal musicians are essentially nerds in black leather. Punk musicians are too, by the way. My leather jacket is fake leather anyhow. Plus, it's always too hot to wear it in Los Angeles.

Certain people were there specifically to hang out with *the stars*. If you were not a *star* they did not want anything to do with you. So you know how at a normal party if you just strike up a conversation with someone they'll usually respond? There wasn't a lot of that. Like, I'd turn and talk to someone and they'd immediately tune me out while looking for a *star* they could concentrate their energies on instead. This behavior was kind of ironic in that had Randy noticed any of them talking to me he might have been more interested in hanging out with them. Which is not to try and beef me up or anything, but a lesson that if you're in a similar situation, kids, you might want to be a little less awestruck of the obvious celebrities.

In any case, I talked for a while with Frank Novenic of Hatebreed. Frank's from Cleveland and was actually impressed to meet an ex-member of Zero Defex. It's not too often that happens! I guess we made some kind of a mark, like a piss stain on a wall. We both knew the late Dave Araca of the Guns.* Frank has a tattoo done by Dave, as do a whole lot of people I know.

So everyone was looking tough, getting drunk, and eating meat,

---

* The Cleveland band, not the LA one.

meat, and more meat while I'm standing there talking Buddhism to one of modern metal's leading lights. It made me really happy to do this because for way too long Buddhism has been the exclusive province of a) whiny intellectuals who try and make it as complicated as possible so no one but their friends can possibly discuss it and b) spaced-out new age waste cases who haven't got a clue what Buddha was on about, but they like that little om symbol. I'm glad to see it reclaimed by normal people. And by "normal people" I mean, of course, booze-soaked heavy metal musicians in leather and studs. Not that Randy himself was booze soaked. His glass was full of nonalcoholic O'Doul's.

Melinda eventually made her way to the barbecue, still very stoned. But by then she'd stopped paying attention to us — or, indeed, to much of anything. Me, though, I mainly stood there wondering, "I'm not stoned. Is this really happening?"

# CHAPTER 19

# ZEN IN SAN QUENTIN

E ven before I'd talked Zen with a bunch of drunken heavy-metal musicians, I'd already talked Zen with thieves and murderers. Let me tell you about that.

Back while I was up there in San Francisco doing the whole San Francisco Zen Center thing, Greg Fain, the guy who'd set that up for me, asked if I'd like to tag along on one of his weekly visits to a group of Buddhist inmates at San Quentin Prison. That sounded pretty weird. So I was game. It seems that the prisoners at San Quentin really like my books. In fact, I've heard this same thing from several people who have contacts in various prisons around the country. Which goes to show you what kind of audience I attract. . . .*

All I knew of prison is what I'd seen in movies — guys rattling their cups on the steel bars of their cells and spending years trying to dig out of the place with soup spoons and stuff like that. I didn't see any of that on my visit, which was a bit of a bummer. But I had fun anyway.

---

\* Hi, guys!

One of the first things I noticed about San Quentin is that it's in an area that's impossibly beautiful out on a little peninsula jutting into the San Francisco Bay. We had to sign in at the gate outside the parking lot, then sign in at the entry gate to the prison itself, where we got our hands stamped and were let into the double set of barred doors that get you into the prison courtyard. Then we had to sign in yet again at another guard station in the courtyard. The courtyard itself is very pretty, with lots of tropical flowers and plants and a little pond with a family of ducks living in it. Although it's a bit austere, nothing in that courtyard would seem out of place in the center of a little Northern California town. Except maybe the ex-murderers in orange jumpsuits.*

You aren't allowed to wear anything orange or made of denim when you go inside San Quentin, since that's what the prisoners wear and they wouldn't want to accidentally machine-gun any of the visitors on their way out. Unfortunately, the only pants I'd brought with me were a pair of jeans, so I had to borrow some sweats from Greg.

Once we were all signed in, we waited outside one of the meeting rooms while the guys started filing out of the prison itself. I'm standing there watching this group of tough-looking dudes in matching denim work shirts hulking toward me, with all their big ol' prisoner mustaches and tattoos. As they got closer, though, I saw that most of them kind of looked like my dad, or at least my dad's friends. The group consisted mainly of middle-aged guys who seemed pretty mellow. Greg had told me earlier that most in the Buddhist group were guys who'd done something really heinous when they were in their twenties and had been here for a couple of decades.

The Zen group meets in the prison's makeshift Muslim chapel, which looks kind of like a third-grade math classroom or something. The guys unlocked some cabinets and took out some *zafus* — round sitting cushions for zazen meditation — and *zabutons* — square

---

\*  Or not...

cushions that go under the round ones so your knees aren't grinding into the floor as you practice. Turns out they'd made the square cushions themselves in the prison workshop.

They set out the cushions and set up a little altar up in front of the room, and we got down to business. First we sat zazen for half an hour, and it was pretty much like any other sitting I've participated in. The Baptists next door had a band getting ready to rock out to some gospel tunes. But the institutional walls were thick enough that the distraction was kept to a minimum. I noticed a few prisoners from other religious denominations wandering by and peering in at us. But everyone was pretty respectful, unlike what you get from passersby at some of the urban Zen centers I've practiced at.

The bell rang to end the sitting, and we had a little break. I talked to some of the guys then. One of them told me he had read all four volumes of Gudo Nishijima's translation of *Shobogenzo* all the way through. Not many of Nishijima's own students have done that, so I was duly impressed. Another guy told me he was interested in Buddhism because of some out-of-body experiences he'd had as a young man. I didn't have the heart to tell him that even though I'd tried desperately in my teens to have one of those, I'd never managed to and that these days I'd rather stay in my own body anyhow.* Pretty soon it was my turn to talk.

Now, what do you say to a bunch of murderers, rapists, and kidnappers — you don't ask specifics, but why else would they be here? — when they want you to talk about Buddhism? I knew that the whole tough punk-rock guy act I can whip out in front of groups of wussy Zen nerds wasn't gonna play in this room. So I talked about a poem called "Inscription of Faith in Mind" by an old Chinese Zen master named Sosan. The poem's most-often quoted sound bite is its first line, which goes, "The Buddhist Way is not difficult to follow,

---

* Actually, in Buddhist terms the idea of an out-of-body experience is absurd, since mind and body are one.

just avoid preferences." Sometimes it's translated, "avoid picking and choosing."*

At any rate, the theme of the poem is that we don't need to fight against the circumstances in which we find ourselves. We have a certain degree of faith that no matter where we find ourselves that's where we really need to be. In fact, no matter how much trouble we may have seeing it, the place where we are could be said to be exactly where we most want to be. This is hard to accept. But when you accept it, your situation changes dramatically. That doesn't mean we should be complacent and accept a bad situation without trying to improve it. In fact, it's one of our duties to improve whatever situation we find ourselves in. To do this effectively, though, first we have to understand that we ourselves are not something apart from our circumstances. *What we are* and *where we are* are one and the same.

I told them the story of how I learned about this in a very practical way. I had a kidney stone a few years ago. I'd had them before. But this time, because your wiring "down there" isn't as precise as it is in your upper body, it felt like someone had smashed my nuts with a ball-peen hammer. I went to the hospital, but they weren't sure what the problem was. Since they thought they might have to do surgery on my family jewels they wouldn't give me any kind of painkillers, not even an aspirin. So as I laid there in horrendous pain I thought, "Okay, Zen Stuff I learned, let's see what you're good for." I decided to feel all the pain without trying to escape from it or compare it to what I wanted to feel like. I would have no preferences. I'd just experience exactly what I was experiencing at that moment. When I did that, the entire thing transformed in a way I can't really describe. Even the concept of "pain" makes no sense unless it's contrasted with something else. When you drop the preference to be without pain, then it's hard to say whether or not pain exists, even if

---

* You can pick and choose your preferred version.

it feels like your bollocks are being crushed by a herd of hippos. Pretty freaky.

Which is not to say I could keep this up for the entire twelve hours or so it took before they decided to give me some medicine, or that I was so "Zen" I said no to the painkillers when they finally offered them. But, still, when I looked at it a different way, the situation utterly changed.

The prison guys seemed able to relate to that. I'm sure they have to deal with a whole big bunch of pain in their day-to-day lives. Still, without being in those circumstances they might never have found zazen. One guy I met told me he did his zazen every morning in his cell. At first, he said, the guys in the cells nearby taunted him and threw crap at him. But he kept right on going. Eventually his determination to practice seemed to impress his neighbors, and they stopped throwing shit. All these guys had a hard time practicing, but they all kept right on going anyway. I had a lot more respect for them than for some of the whiners who show up at my place and complain that a half hour of zazen practice is *too hard*. Oh, boo-hoo-hoo!

Greg and I had come to San Quentin along with a couple of women who also volunteered for these prison outreach Zen gigs. One of them was moving away and wouldn't be able to attend the prison Zen stuff after that day. At the end of the practice the guys presented her with a beautiful miniature Buddhist altar they'd made in the prison woodshop. It was one of the most touching gestures I'd ever witnessed.

I left San Quentin thinking I'd just met some of the most dedicated practitioners of Zen I'll probably ever encounter in my life. While it's not always necessary to practice in the kind of adversity these guys face, it's inspirational to know that people practice under some unfathomably difficult circumstances.

## CHAPTER 20

# *CANNED!*

**W**hen I got out of San Quentin,* I found another little surprise waiting for me. An email from one of my bosses — the older one, Mr. Miyagi, for those of you keeping score at home — had arrived while I was in transit. In stilted and formal Japanese it said that the management had decided to shut down the company's operations in the US. This time it was clear they didn't mean just moving me out of the office building I was in, since I wasn't in one anymore. The email was worded as if the company actually had some "operations in the United States" other than me pissing around in my apartment. Further instructions would be forthcoming, it said.

Super.

It's not like this news was exactly unexpected. But it came at the worst possible time. Many months earlier I'd accepted an invitation to be a guest teacher at the Great Sky Zen Sesshin in southern Minnesota, and it was just about to start. While I was there I wouldn't be reachable by email or telephone for ten days.

---

* I like the sound of that. Makes me seem tough.

Ultrasuper.

So let me tell you about Great Sky. Doing zazen when you're stuck in prison is a noble thing. But there are folks who deliberately place themselves in close to prisonlike conditions just so they can practice some intensive Zen. It's called a *sesshin*, pronounced "seh-sheen."

So, you may ask, what's a *sesshin?* For one thing it is not a *session*. I hate it when people say "Zen session" as if it's like a jam session or something. The word *sesshin* is not one of those English words that the Japanese have modified into one of their own, like *beisuboru* for baseball or *sekusu purey* for sex play. It's a legitimate Japanese word and is spelled out in Chinese characters like this: 接心. The first character means "to gather together," "organize," or "clean up." The second one means "mind" or "heart." So a *sesshin* is a special elongated zazen practice period intended to let you get your heart and mind back together. And remember, in Buddhism we don't make a distinction between body and heart/mind. So a *sesshin* includes a lot of physical practice as well.

*Sesshins* typically last three, five, or seven days. Sometimes you'll find longer ones and sometimes shorter. Attendees spend between four and six hours a day doing zazen practice. Meals are served in a formal style with a lot of chanting and some very specific rules as to how utensils are handled, how bowls are cleaned, when you have to stop eating, and so forth. The idea is that even meals become Zen practice.

When you're not doing zazen or eating you're usually engaged in work practice, which is called *samu* in Japanese. *Samu* is a very important part of any *sesshin* and may range from simple chores like mopping floors or cleaning toilets to large-scale operations like building or clearing land. Generally, though, the workload is not too intense.

Also, *sesshins* cost money. For reasons I've never been able to fathom, this particular point always seems to hang up some people.

Even when the cost per day of a *sesshin* that includes accommodations, meals, and Zen training works out to way less than you'd ever pay for a hotel that didn't serve you meals or offer any kind of training, certain people will inevitably complain about having to pay.

The reason a *sesshin* costs money for the participants is because it costs money for the organizers. You gotta rent the space; buy the food; get all the toilet paper, cleaning supplies, and whatnot people will use; arrange transportation; all kinds of stuff. So stop bitching because you have to fork over some dough to enjoy what's been prepared for you.

Most *sesshins* have one teacher. The Great Sky Sesshin is unique in that it is attended by several teachers. In 2007 there were six of us: Tonen O'Connor of the Milwaukee Zen Center; Zuiko Redding of the Cedar Rapids Zen Center; Dokai Georgeson of Hokyoji, the place where we were holding the *sesshin*; Rosan Yoshida of the Missouri Zen Center; Genmyo Smith of the Prairie Zen Center in Champaign, Illinois; and me. Tonen and Zuiko are women. The rest of us teachers were guys.

La Crosse Airport in Wisconsin is the nearest airport to Hokyoji monastery. Hokyoji is officially in Eitzen, Minnesota, but it's actually nearer to New Albin, Iowa, a hamlet that houses about two hundred people, including a guy whose real name is Jug Darling, who's run the local gas station for the past thirty or so years. You get to Hokyoji via an unpaved gravel road that leads you to a mile-long driveway into the place itself. There's electricity and running water at Hokyoji. But the sewer system doesn't extend all the way out to the monastery, so what comes into Hokyoji stays there until someone comes and takes it away.

Dokai, the guy who runs Hokyoji, showed up at the airport and took me to the monastery in his mom's Lincoln Town Car. Any guy who drives his mom's car is cool by me. When we got to Hokyoji, it was about 700 degrees and 1,000,000 percent humidity. Even so, Tonen and Zuiko were already decked out in their full Zen robes and sweating profusely. I'd known Tonen for a while. One of the first out-of-town speaking gigs I ever did was at the Milwaukee Zen Center, which she runs. Her teacher, Tozen* Akiyama, became interested in Zen while he was a merchant marine in the fifties because he was always being asked about it. Like most Japanese people, he didn't know zip about Zen, so he decided to find out. Eventually he became ordained as a teacher. He ended up in Milwaukee, where he met Tonen, who at the time was Sara O'Connor, a director of nonprofit theater productions. Tonen's travels with theater groups had already led her to Japan and to her own encounters with Zen. When Tozen left the Milwaukee Zen Center he put Tonen in charge.

Tonen's friend Zuiko, like Tonen, looked like a typical midwestern mom, only with a shaved head and a set of Buddhist robes. I took a liking to Zuiko instantly. I'm not really sure why. You just know that some people are cool right when you meet them. Zuiko had studied for a short time with Shundo Aoyama, a female Zen teacher in Japan known for her strict attention to the details of monastic dress and ceremonies. But Zuiko's main teacher was a guy named Tsugen Narasaki. Narasaki, like Nishijima, was interested in the real practice of zazen rather than in the ceremonial stuff most Japanese Zen teachers are concerned with. Even so, because of her study with Shundo Aoyama, Zuiko knew all the Zen protocol backward and forward. Yet she still seemed unfazed by my rather atypical mode of dress.

I came to the retreat in an *Invasion of the Saucer Men* T-shirt. I feel comfortable and normal in T-shirts. When I wear Zen robes I feel like a guy at a Halloween party dressed as a monk. Besides, I start sweating like a pig the moment I even think about putting them on. And on a day like this I didn't even want to let such thoughts cross my mind.

---

* That's To-ZEN; his student is To-NEN. Often Dharma names given in a specific Zen lineage sound alike. All Nishijima's dharma heirs' dharma names end in "do," for example. Mine is Odo.

The first night at the Great Sky Sesshin was just instructions on how to eat dinner and then one round of zazen. During the evening zazen I could hear a massive thunderstorm way off in the distance. Lights-out was at 9:00 p.m., which was 6 p.m. in California. Ugh. The thunderstorm finally hit us good and hard at 11:30. Rain slammed against the windows like machine-gun bullets while the reconverted workshop where I was staying with several other guys creaked and rocked in the wind. An hour later it was over. But there would be plenty more where that came from.

When the bell ringers came by for the 4:30 a.m. wake-up call the following morning I got my first look at the Great Sky from which the *sesshin* takes its name. Far from any sources of light pollution, distant gas nebulas and the Milky Way stood out clearly against the velvet-without-Elvis-painted-on-it blackness of space. Some stars even glowed with faint colors. It looked like the sky you'd see from a planet near the center of the galaxy where the stars are all crammed close. But this was planet earth. This was the way the night sky was supposed to look from our world.

I slogged through the mud up to the zendo to begin the first day of seven days of intensive zazen practice. This was to be my first *sesshin* longer than four days. Nishijima believes that long *sesshins* are actually detrimental to practice, since they're so different from daily sitting at home. He limited his to four days maximum. Even with twenty-five years of daily zazen under my belt I wondered if I could survive a seven-day *sesshin* without going insane.

Dogen said that in zazen you were to "think the thought of not thinking." When asked what this meant he said, "It's different from thinking." Be that as it may, I had a lot of things buzzing around in my head when I arrived. My mom was dead, my job was beyond ridiculous, my marriage seemed to be over and done for, I wondered if I'd be able to see Shizuko again, and I was head of a Buddhist organization that several members didn't want me to be head of. Before arriving I had decided that by the time the week was over I needed to be clear about what direction my life was going in next. I may not be able to work out all the specifics, I figured. But at least I needed to get some sense of where I was going.

I imagine that a normal person faced with death, job loss, and impending divorce who decided to work things out would do so by thinking very, very hard about it. I know this is the tactic I would have pursued before I'd done all that zazen practice.

But Buddhists believe that the solution to any problem we face is always *here*. We just cover it over with thought. My first Zen teacher used to say that the best way to deal with any problem was to sit with it. Well, I had seven days to sit with these problems. And that's what I was determined to do.

I would not consciously attempt to find a solution by manipulating words and images in my brain. Instead, I would let those words and images gradually untangle themselves until the solution that already existed became clear. Or so I hoped.

Now, I know that Zen practice is supposed to be goalless. And I know that having a goal for a *sesshin* is pretty ridiculous. But we humans often do ridiculous things. I didn't know or even care very much whether I achieved the goal I set for myself. But I knew from past experiences that long zazen sittings could help things like these become clearer.

My legs were already in agony by eight in the morning of day one — by which time I'd already been doing zazen for three hours, mind you. Why did I ever sign up for this? If there was any solution to my problems I wasn't seeing it. My mind was just full of muck. Not a single thing was clear. It was just a load of noise and distortion.

Each teacher at Great Sky was scheduled for one day as *doshi*, the practice leader, the dude or dudette in charge of things. I was scheduled to be the *doshi* on day four. I did my best to watch the other teachers as they performed the various rituals I'd be expected to perform in a few days. At Nishijima's retreats, the only thing the leader did was put some incense in the burner, light it up, and do three prostrations to the Buddha each morning. At Great Sky the *doshi* was expected to do a whole bunch of rituals. There were chanting ceremonies that needed leading, ritualized incense offerings way more complex than any I'd ever done, loads of bowing, more chanting ceremonies. I'd never done any of this before.

At a *sesshin*, the teacher will often make him- or herself available for private consultation and instruction with the participants. This is called *dokusan* in the Soto tradition and *sanzen* in the Rinzai tradition. In Soto, *dokusan* is usually voluntary, but in Rinzai, *sanzen* is generally mandatory for all participants. In both traditions the usual deal is that the teacher rings a bell, the participant comes into the room, bows are made, and the talk begins. Depending on the style of the teacher these may be fairly informal chats or highly ritualized encounters in which the participant is expected to present his or her understanding of the practice to the teacher. Generally speaking, in the Soto tradition you're more likely to encounter the former, while in the Rinzai tradition you're more likely to encounter the latter. At Great Sky, each teacher was expected to do *dokusan* on his or her day as *doshi*.

I'd only done *dokusan* once, and that was as a student. I'd never done it as a teacher. I had no idea how *dokusan* was supposed to be handled here at Great Sky, so I signed myself up for a couple as a student before I had to do them as a teacher.

The first *dokusan* I did on the first day with Zuiko was nice. Her teacher didn't do *dokusan* either, so she was as green to it as me. We just chatted about stuff. She was fascinated by the fact that I was what she called a "transmitted layperson." By that she meant that although I'd received dharma transmission from my teacher I was not a monastic.

I told her that Nishijima never made any clear distinction between laypeople and monks. To him, anyone who took the Buddhist precepts was a monk, and anyone who accepted the precepts was eligible for dharma transmission. This isn't the way it works in most places. There's generally a clear distinction between laypeople and monks. There are all kinds of extra ceremonies and levels of monastic training to go through for monks.

But here's something important I don't want to pass over. Although some of us Zen weirdos don't care a whole lot about the ceremonial stuff, ceremony and ritual are a vital and indispensable part of Zen practice. Let me just write that again just so you don't miss it. I said there is no Zen without ceremony and ritual.

A lot of people who come to my Zen classes are shocked when I chant a sutra or even — gasp! — show up wearing my dreaded black Buddhist robes. I don't do it a lot. But I do it some. If you got rid of all the ceremonies and rituals, what you'd be left with would not be Buddhism. More on that later.

Zuiko was nice and encouraged me to pursue my unique style of teaching and practice. But I could tell she didn't like the fact that a teacher at Great Sky Sesshin wasn't wearing the regulation clothes. She didn't say anything specific. I could just tell. She was gonna get me later, though.

# CHAPTER 21

## AIN'T GOT NOTHIN' YET

*I* didn't notice the gigantic spider under the toilet seat until I was done with my morning poop. But when I went to pour lime into the muck, as we'd been told to do after doing our number-twos, there she was, big, black, hairy, and potentially poisonous. I hoped she understood that the smelly poo that had just whizzed past her nest was bound to attract more flies for her to eat. I figured that's why she set up shop there to begin with.

The outhouses at Hokyoji were not the most disgusting toilets I'd ever used. Those were the toilets at Ozzfest. But still, I'm not a camping kinda guy. I can't recall the last time I had to make use of toilets where your dumpings just went into a big pile at the bottom of a hole in the dirt.

Anyway, I made it to the zendo on time and without getting bit by the spider, so day two of the Great Sky Sesshin was off to a good start.

I hadn't figured out what I was gonna do with my life during the first day. Not that I expected any kind of definitive Answer to show up in my head. Though that would've been nice! But it wasn't gonna happen, and I knew it. I just continued to let stuff come up out of my brain as it wanted to. I spent the prebreakfast zazen rounds pretty unfocused and muddy. Every morning at the end of the second round of zazen they rang a bell outside the zendo twenty times to signal that the sun had risen. In ancient days Buddhist temples were the center of village life, just like churches were in the West. In the pre—alarm clock era the temple bells woke the townsfolk up for work.

There was no town within earshot of Hokyoji. But old traditions die hard. The bells provided an unexpected diversion for me. My thoughts were racing around so fast that I tried to see if I could just stay completely focused on the practice for the twenty or thirty seconds between each ring. No luck at all.

I can remember my very first all-day sit at Tim's place. At the time I was trying to decide on a new guitar to buy. The $300 I'd allotted was damn hard to come by. I had to get an instrument that would be able to play any kind of music I might be called on to perform. I spent the entire day's zazen pondering which of several instruments I'd looked at in the previous week to get. I envisioned how each instrument would look and sound. I considered all the possible bands I might join. By the end of the day my mind was made up.

Of all the hundreds of day-long zazens I've done, this is the only one where I can clearly recall what I was thinking about at the time. I knew I wasn't really supposed to be pondering stuff like that. Maybe that's why I remember it so well. Or maybe because I later came to really regret getting the piece-of-shit guitar I ended up choosing.

These days I'm far less likely to deliberately churn stuff around in my head like that. Even though I wasn't purposely bringing them up, the issues seemed so pressing that whenever my brain got a little quiet, something inside would send one of them up to the surface, and I'd lock onto it before I even realized what I was doing. As soon as I did notice I was doing that I'd stop adding energy to it, and the thought would fade away. Even so, there was always another thought right on its tail.

It never does you any good to try and forcibly stop your thoughts. Your attempts at forcing thoughts to stop can sometimes seem effective. But all you're really doing is introducing a new thought that's louder than the old one. Repetitive, hypnotizing thoughts like mantras or koans are especially effective in creating and sustaining the illusion that you've transcended thought. But all you've actually managed is to focus on one specific thought. This still doesn't solve the real problem, which is your habitual practice of focusing on thought itself.

I got through breakfast, and after a short break it was back to the cushion. This time things were a bit easier, but not spectacularly so. Then, all at once during the sitting right before lunch, my third book — the book you are reading this very second — was revealed. I don't mean to imply that I saw the book laid out for me on the white wall I'd been staring at for the past several hours. But even if I had, it couldn't have been any clearer. I was gonna expose everything. The Zen Death Trip, the crap with Nakano Productions, the stupid hassles with Dogen Sangha, how Yuka told me I wasn't a man to her anymore, how I'd fucked Shizuko as a reaction to that, how I wanted to fuck my student Leilani too, how my mom got burned up in a big pizza oven, the whole damned thing. It would be the book that destroyed once and forever any myths anyone could hold about what Zen masters were or should be. In its place would be a real-life warts-and-all portrait of what a Zen teacher in the twenty-first century actually is.

I knew I would fail at this. People who wanted to keep their belief in gurus and perfected masters would hold on tight to their illusions. For them all my talk about my own failings would only be evidence that I wasn't as fully enlightened as their great heroes. Fuck 'em. Maybe a few people out there would get it, and that would be enough.

I still couldn't be absolutely certain if I'd been fired. Nakano Productions could conceivably ask me to come back to Japan or maybe go work at their branch office in Seoul or something. But I decided that either way it was time to quit the company. Twelve years ago I thought I'd finally found my dream job, the one I'd never tire of. I had visions of making Zone Robo a huge hit in America. Who better to make their show the success it deserved to be than a guy who'd made his way all the way from Akron, Ohio, to Tokyo just to fulfill his dream of making that happen?

But that wasn't going to happen. It had been perfectly clear at the meeting in May that the company was no longer in any state to do what needed to be done to make their shows successful in the West. Nothing I could do was going to change that. Now with their decision to shut down their Los Angeles operations, there was nothing left for me to do, even nominally. And I wasn't going to waste my time on such nonsense.

But more than that, I had a duty in North America. I know I'm gonna make half my readers throw their books across the room in disgust when I say this.* There was no other Buddhist teacher like me in America. And gosh darn it all, someone like me was *absolutely necessary*. And too bad if you don't like hearing that.

The revelation passed, and I let it go.

Later on during one of the breaks Zuiko took me aside and very politely said, "I wish you'd wear your robes." Shit. If you say it nicely, now I have to do it. So I went back up to my room and put my robes on over my T-shirt and shorts. This is strictly nonregulation, by the way. Real Buddhist robes are a whole outfit right down to the underwear. But it was way over 90 that day, and there was no way anybody was gonna get me into all that stuff.

I sat there for the afternoon zazen sessions with rivers of ripe-smelling sweat flowing from every pore in my body, while next to me Genmyo Smith of the Prairie Zen Center sat stock-still in

---

* You're on page 132, by the way, just in case later you decide to pick the book back up and start reading again.

full robes looking cool as a daikon radish. I kept wondering how he survived.

Moksha, a tall, lanky woman attending the *sesshin* who'd done a load of Zen retreats before, was going to be my helper in a couple of days when I had to handle the leadership chores. She kindly wrote little notes all over one of the booklets that had the chants printed in it to show when I was supposed to bow or light incense and other stuff.

I went to bed with at least one of my problems worked out. But there were a lot more to go. That night I had a vivid lucid dream — a lucid dream is the kind of dream when you realize you're dreaming and you can do whatever you want. It was so real I remember thinking during the dream, "I'd better get some sleep because I have to get up early tomorrow." Then I realized I was already asleep, so it didn't matter.

In the dream I was standing in a field of pine-green grass. There was a child playing nearby who I recognized from old photos as my father at about age four. I told him, "This is a dream." He said he knew. I asked him what he wanted to do, thinking he'd want to take advantage of the fact that we could do anything, since it was a dream. But he didn't want to fly or shoot laser beams out of his fingertips. He wanted to ride a bike. I asked him how long ago this was, since his age meant I'd gone back in time. "About a week ago, I guess," he said. I laughed and said it was a lot longer ago than that.

I don't recall anything else about the dream. I still don't really have any clear idea what it meant. I used to have tons of lucid dreams when I first started doing zazen. In fact, it got to be kind of a problem after a while, and I was glad when they stopped. When you start loosening up the stuff in your brain that's the kind of thing that can happen.

A few days later I talked to Dokai, the guy who runs Hokyoji, about it. He said that when he first got to Hokyoji, he used to have lots of lucid dreams. Eventually he started doing zazen in his dreams. Why didn't I ever think of that?

When I was walking to the zendo for the 5 a.m. zazen the next day I heard a train whistle far, far away. It was the first sound of human civilization outside the monastery I'd heard since I arrived. So the real world *was* still out there. Zazen was a little better that day. But I did start composing my resignation letter to Nakano Productions during one of the midmorning sittings. Once I noticed I was doing that, though, I stopped pretty quickly and got back to business. The rest of day three continued in a pretty similar way to day two, but with no new revelations.

The next day would be my day to lead the practice and do *dokusan*. In my notebook I wrote, "I'm certain I will fuck everything up."

# CHAPTER 22

# *THUNDER ON THE PRAIRIE*

Another colossal thunderstorm rolled through the night before it was my turn to be practice leader. Raindrops as big and heavy as marbles tried to shatter the windows, while lightning strikes as bright as a flashbulb in your face came almost simultaneously with thunder cracks so loud the building wobbled like a fat man on a trampoline. Several of the attendants at the *sesshin* were staying in tents pitched on the lawn rather than in the buildings. I wondered how they were managing. The previous night there'd been talk that if the storm we could see rolling in over the hills got too bad they could sleep in the zendo. I hoped they made it. But I wasn't about to run outside and check.

By the morning wake-up bell the deluge had passed. Today was my day to do a lot of the ritual and ceremonial stuff that makes Buddhism look like a religion. But one reason we have these rituals is because although Buddhism isn't a religion, it's also not atheism. Atheism is a big trend in America these days.

Let me try and explain the difference between Buddhism and atheism. I'll do it badly. But here goes.

Buddhism does not have any creator God. There's no idea that some giant white man with a beard made the universe a long time ago. Nor is there any idea that some super being sits around somewhere* outside the universe watching over it and intervening whenever he feels things have gotten out of hand, or when he just wants a certain football team to score a touchdown.

Buddha is not a supernatural being. We don't worship him. Nor do we worship any of the other beings you read about in the sutras like Avalokiteshvara or Manjushri or any of the rest of those guys.

But that doesn't mean Buddhists reject the existence of God. Different Buddhists express it in different ways. Joshu Sasaki, a teacher in the Rinzai tradition of Zen, likes to say, "There is no God, and He is your creator." Gudo Nishijima says, "God is the Universe, and the Universe is God."

Although we don't worship Buddha, we still do prostrations to statues of him. We recite poems to these statues and light candles and offer incense to them. We even put food in front of the statues at mealtimes during retreats. So what's up with that?

We don't really believe that Buddha is somehow encased within these statues and that he receives our offerings or magically eats the food. Nor do we believe that he's sitting up there in nirvana listening to the stuff we chant at these statues. We don't believe he's going to grant us any favors for acknowledging him or that he might get pissed off at us if we fail to accord him the proper respect.

But as I mentioned earlier, all those prostrations, chants, incense offerings, and the rest have an undeniable psychological and physical effect. Even though we may not know where our need for this kind of action comes from, we need to acknowledge it exists. It's just as strong in any atheist as it is in any religious fanatic. Atheists want to throw away everything about religion, including the stuff that

*   Where?

clearly fulfills a real human need. That's never gonna fly. We need certain aspects of religion to make us feel right.

Today it was my duty to lead everyone at Great Sky through the Zen Buddhist version of those necessary rituals. I knew how to chant a sutra; I'd chanted the Heart Sutra when they shoved my dead mom into the big pizza oven. I knew how to do prostrations. I'd offered incense before. I'd done pretty much everything I was required to do. But I'd never done it all in the proper sequence in front of paying customers.

Moksha was a big help. Maybe too big of a help. She was constantly "pssst-ing" and poking my shoulder to let me know what had to be done next. But it didn't really matter all that much if I got all the steps just right. As long as I did something fairly close, it was fine. Most people there had no idea what I was doing, and even if they did, they all had their backs turned to me anyway. So I got through it okay.

This was also my day to deliver the dharma talk. I had something vaguely prepared about the true nature of a teacher in the Zen tradition. But I mostly ignored my notes and winged it. People seemed okay with what I said. I got a couple of laughs. I tend to judge my success as a speaker by how many laughs I get.

I got a few interesting questions from the audience. One guy asked how to prevent having expectations in Zen practice. But anyone doing this practice is going to have expectations. You expect to achieve peace of mind. You expect to deepen your understanding. You expect to get enlightenment. If you were me at that *sesshin*, you'd expect to solve your work and marriage problems. There's no way to stop having expectations. The best you can do is to understand that your expectations will never be realized. My own expectations about my life were certainly not being realized this year. But that didn't really matter. Just know that your expectations are only thoughts in your head, and keep on doing what you do.

Someone else asked why Buddha never talked about pain in practice, when obviously the practice was pretty damned painful. Dokai chimed in with a good answer to that. In Buddha's day even the most basic things we take for granted now were, by our standards, at least, really painful. There were no cars or trains, and even travel by horse was reserved mainly for the wealthy. So wherever you went you had to walk. Medicine hadn't developed as far as it has now. If you had a backache you couldn't just run across the street and buy some Tylenol. Plus, many of what we consider minor ailments could be devastating or deadly. There was no such thing as mosquito spray. No such thing as air conditioning. Even for the most well-to-do, life was pretty rough. In that milieu, the aches you get from sitting zazen for a little while probably seemed too trivial to be worthy of commenting on.

Pain is part of our practice. Zazen is not meant to be the most comfortable way to spend half an hour. It's a practice of body and mind, so the body must be engaged.. In order to practice Zen you need to be fully aware of your body. This is also why the eyes are open during zazen practice. When you shut your eyes you're shutting out the outside world and saying that the inner world of your own mind is more important. The Zen attitude is that both the inner subjective world and the outer objective world should be absolutely equal.

I got through the lecture and the lunch service. But following that, it was time for my very first *dokusan*, one-on-one meetings with students. I was pretty nervous.

My first customer was a middle-aged woman who asked what to do about all the spinning wheels in her head during zazen. In my talk I'd said that what usually goes on in our heads is kinda like if we had a room with a bunch of bicycles turned upside down resting on their handlebars, and we keep spinning the wheels. Every time we notice that one wheel has slowed down, we run over and give it another big spin. This is how we normally deal with our thoughts. We habitually try to keep a steady stream of noise going in our heads. The instant it settles down a little we try and find something exciting to get the brain cells churning again. This is such a deeply ingrained habit for most of us that we have no idea we're even doing it.

I told her that just realizing you're doing this isn't enough to make it stop. You need to develop new habits. And that's what the practice is for. Each time you catch yourself spinning one of those wheels, you stop doing it. The momentum you've already added to the wheel won't stop instantly just because you stopped spinning it. But give it time, and it will settle down of its own accord.

Next up was a young guy who was very serious about his practice. He tried to do everything with the greatest possible efficiency, he said. I understand that. I have that mind-set myself. If I'm not doing something productive I feel like I'm just wasting time. This is one of the reasons Zen practice has been really good for me. It allows me to relax while still feeling I'm not just wasting time, which is how I'd feel if I did most of the things normal people do to relax. He seemed like he was on the right track but maybe pushing things a bit too much. I told him not to worry so much or work so hard.

My next customer was an interesting case. She was born in Israel and converted from Judaism to Catholicism in her twenties because she found it more reasonable and attractive, but now she was fed up with Catholicism and was looking to Buddhism for the answers she sought. She told me she was no stranger to spiritual practice. She came to the retreat to see if Buddhism would really give her what she was looking for.

She talked a lot about spiritual practice. But I told her I didn't think Buddhism was a spiritual practice. If you need to classify everything as either spiritual or secular, then Buddhism certainly isn't secular. So I can accept it being called spiritual in that sense. But Buddhism is something a little different from what we usually think of as spiritual practice. Spiritual religions like Judaism and Catholicism, generally speaking, emphasize the supposedly divine aspect of our nature over and above the material aspect. The same is true of Eastern spiritual traditions. But Buddhism says that spirit and matter are manifestations of the same underlying reality, which is neither spirit nor matter. When we emphasize one over the other we miss half of reality. It's every bit as illusory to languish in spirituality as it is to wallow in materialism.

Next up was a young woman who told me she'd suffered from panic attacks in the past and hoped that Zen might be of some help. This I could relate to. I've had a few big panic attacks and a number of minor ones myself. I wrote about one of these in detail in my first book.

I told her that in Zen practice the many psychological barriers we maintain to shield ourselves from aspects of our own personalities that we don't care for can begin to break down. This can be very disturbing if you're not prepared for it. It's not likely this will be really bad unless your practice is very ambitious and goal directed. This is one of many reasons I'm so against Zen practice that's specifically geared toward acquiring so-called enlightenment experiences. Some of what ends up getting defined by dodgy Zen masters as enlightenment experiences are really nothing more than panic attacks or nervous breakdowns. The practice could help her, I said. She just had to be careful not to push for "results." I also told her to maintain contact with her teacher who could help her if anything weird should happen in her practice.

My final *dokusan* was with a woman who had traveled all the way from Hungary just to attend the Great Sky Sesshin. She found my style of teaching annoying, she said. My attitude toward ceremonies struck her as immature. She was also unimpressed by the way I kept referring to things my teacher had told me. This, she said, was another sign of my lack of maturity.

You can't please everyone, I suppose. And I'm probably not the world's greatest walking advertisement for what a mature person ought to look like. But I don't really think the fact that Zen teachers often reference their own teachers is necessarily a sign of immaturity. Buddhism is still essentially an oral tradition. What we hear from our teachers forms the real basis for our understanding far more than the things we read. But no matter how well you might memorize what your teachers have said, the interpretation of what you've heard is unique to you alone.

As for my attitude toward robes and ceremonies, maybe it is immature. But I still hate those damned robes, and I was dying to get out of them as soon as possible. After she was done roasting me my turn as practice leader was over and I was a step closer to getting my wish. I got to return to the zendo and finish out the day pretty much as a regular attendee except for having to sit at the front of the room. No more ceremonies to lead. Relief at last.

## CHAPTER 23

# *IN WHICH I HAVE TO TAKE A PEE REALLY BAD*

In the middle of the next day of the retreat I had to pee like a motherfucker. During the work period I'd drunk a couple of jugs full of water to try and keep hydrated in the massive heat while I was spreading woodchips along the base of every tree on the Hoky-oji grounds. I didn't want to give myself another kidney stone way the hell out in the middle of the woods. I'd gone to the toilet just before zazen. But the very second I hit the cooler air of the zendo I started having to take a whiz again. The zazen period would be forty minutes. I had a choice to make. It was perfectly acceptable to get up and leave as long as you weren't too obtrusive. But I figured I'd tough it out until the bell rang. Soon, though, the coolness of the zendo made my kidneys continue to pump more water into my bladder until by halfway into the sitting it was almost unbearably painful.

Still I decided to tough it out. This is not behavior I encourage, by the way. Dogen said you should never try to hold your pee when sitting. So even he would have forgiven me if I'd gotten up and left early. Yet I chose to ignore the sage advice of the great man himself.

The period was more than halfway over already. I figured I could make it.

As I sat there in agony my mind started racing. What was wrong with the guy who's supposed to ring the bell? It had to have been two hours since we started! Had he died? Maybe he was dead! Maybe he died on his cushion and nobody noticed. If I went and checked on him and found out he was dead I'd be a hero. I'd ring the bell and we could all leave and I could finally take a piss. He had to be dead.

I checked my watch. It had been twenty-eight minutes. Oh, Jesus God. Could I make it for another twelve? I decided I could. This was hell. . . .

At last the bell rang, and I hightailed it to the outhouse and let loose with a ten-minute piss. The incident seemed to encapsulate a lot about how Zen retreats always seem to go for me. So let me tell you about that.

One of the most interesting things I noticed on the first few Zen retreats I attended was how prolonged zazen can make even your most profound or scariest or sexiest or grossest or otherwise in-any-way-interesting thoughts seem about as intriguing as watching paint dry. After a while it's like a wad of gum in your mouth from which all the flavor has been chewed. No matter how many times you turn those thoughts over and over and over in your brain, they just have no taste anymore.

When what you are doing *is* essentially watching the paint dry on the walls in front of you for hours and hours on end, your brain gets to work digging out whatever it can find to try and keep itself occupied — kind of like a lazy employee pretending to work because the boss is watching. You'd be amazed what's stored up in your head. It's like rummaging through an attic where you've been tossing all your unmentionables for decades. There's old comic books, pictures of your ex-girlfriend, a piano riff from a record by Harry Belafonte you didn't even remember you owned. There are bad movies they showed you in grade school, there are minor childhood traumas you suffered at the hands of cousins you haven't seen in years, there's the light switch in the house you used to live in back in 1987. Then there's other stuff — deeper, darker stuff. Stuff that's so alien to your conscious mind you can't even identify it as "you" the way you can with most of your thoughts. All this junk just keeps coming up like a toilet overflowing and tossing out the remnants of TV dinners you ate three weeks ago.

For a while that process might be interesting. But after a couple of days there's nothing else fun or even creepy in there you haven't seen a hundred times before. No matter what your brain tosses up at you, it's just more *stuff*, and you don't really even care anymore. At this point, though, you're also getting well and truly fed up with being on this stupid Zen retreat. You have no idea what in God's name ever made you even consider signing up for such a thing. But now you're stuck here, way the hell out in the middle of the woods with a bunch of nerds who think it's really cool to be all "Zen" and shit for a week. Fucking assholes. Why don't they just all go die?

You start planning escapes. Maybe you can claim you're feeling ill and get a ride back to civilization. No. Can't wimp out in front of a bunch of Zen nerds! Maybe you can deliberately injure yourself during the work period. "Accidentally" cut a tendon with a garden hoe or something. Yeah. That'd be better than doing more of this shit! It would hurt a lot. But maybe it'd be worth it. No. There's gotta be a better way. Carve your soap into the shape of a gun and threaten the head teacher with it unless he shuts the fuck up and does exactly what you say. Slowly now. No false moves. . . .

Shit. No. Gotta stay the course. Gotta see the thing through. So you get back to it. How many more days now? And how many hours does that work out to? And how many minutes? Shit. Why did I do this to myself?

You think nobody else feels like this. But they all do.

After a while of this, though, you start to reach a certain spot. I can't really tell you what the spot is exactly, or how to reach it. But it feels real good just to stay right there. You've been looking into a mirror the whole time. Not literally, of course. But in a way that's exactly what zazen is. You like what you see sometimes. But a lot of times you don't. Still, you keep facing it down and facing it down. Finally you realize you can live with it. It isn't as great as you wish it was, but it isn't as awful as you feared it might be. It's just what it is. It's the universe. And it's you. And it's cool. Very fucking cool.

I got to that spot in the sitting after the nightmare pee session. The pain in my legs and lower back couldn't possibly stand up to what I'd just experienced. Hurt all you want, legs! Ha! Sometime during that sitting it occurred to me that if I had thoughts or didn't have thoughts, if my sitting seemed great or if my sitting seemed lousy, if I had to pee or didn't have to pee, none of that mattered at all. Zazen transcends whether you think it's going well or going lousy. No matter how you feel about it, the practice is still exactly what it is.

Retreats can be a great way to learn real patience. If you can sit and wait for the bell to ring signaling the end of another interminable round when you're sure the guy who's job it was to ring the bell died six hours ago you can sit patiently through pretty much anything life throws at you.

A *sesshin* can also teach you fearlessness. There is no greater fear than your fear of facing yourself. You might think that the things that scare you most come from outside you. But they never do. When you can face down your own fear of yourself, nothing anyone else does can ever scare you again. Oh, they might startle or surprise you. Nothing can fix that. But no one can truly scare you anymore.

Finally Friday came. The retreat was over. This didn't fill me with great joy because as soon as I got back home I had a mountain of trouble to deal with. The rain had been steady and pretty heavy since the middle of the previous night. Little rivers were starting to form in depressions in the field between the zendo and the house. I'd never seen rain like this, even during typhoons in Japan. Sure, those were harder and heavier, but they let up after a few hours. This just went on and on and on.

We were supposed to end the retreat with a memorial service for Katagiri Roshi, the founder of the monastery, at his gravesite up on the hill above the zendo. But it was way too wet for that, so we had the service inside the zendo. Each participant was supposed to offer incense and say a few words. It was a cute little ceremony.

Later, after all the other participants had gone home, I asked Dokai if I could use his phone to check on my plane reservations. It was lucky I did. My plane to Los Angeles had been canceled! The rain wasn't that bad. I guess they just didn't have enough customers so they changed my flight to the following day. Dokai said I could stay at the cabin until the next day. This would give me another twenty-four hours to avoid facing all the shit I had to face.

Dokai and I went out to breakfast the next morning in nearby Lansing, Iowa, the closest real town to Hokyoji. The buffet was full of fatty foods, including deep-fried pickles. No wonder so many of the people I saw on the streets were so enormous. We set out for the airport and found that the main road had been washed out. Then we found that the detour road was also buried under a mudslide. Railroad tracks had been destroyed in a number of areas when the ground underneath them had been swept into the Mississippi River. This was some hella weather! We finally found another route to the airport. By then I was already half an hour late for the plane. Lucky for me the plane was delayed two hours! After a long, circuitous flight involving numerous airline changes, I finally made it back to Los Angeles. My suitcase, however, did not. This was the least of my troubles.

# CHAPTER 24

# PSYCHO KITTY, QU'EST QUE C'EST?

From a quiet Zen retreat in the wilds of southern Minnesota I went straight back to smelly, polluted, overcrowded Los Angeles to face my job mess, my marriage mess, and all the other messes in my messy life.

My work situation hadn't changed in the time I'd been away. Everything was still stagnant. As far as I could tell no one back in Tokyo had even noticed I'd been gone for ten days. It turns out they had a whole lot more on their minds that week than me. But I wouldn't find out the full extent of that for another few weeks. At the time it just seemed like they were ignoring me and I didn't know why. But I was still getting paid. So I guess that was good.

Once I got home I sat down with Yuka and told her my decisions. It wasn't easy to do. But somehow it wasn't hard either. It was what needed doing, so I just did it. I'd decided that no matter what happened I was quitting Nakano Productions and moving away from Los Angeles. Without the job at Nakano how could I afford to continue in this place? I figured maybe I'd go up to Montreal and see if

I could make some kind of a living there on a combination of the trickle that was coming in from my writing and whatever day job I could get there. I didn't know if Shizuko would be happy with my intention to move there or not. We weren't really any kind of a couple. But at the very least she'd be one more person I knew up in the Great White North. I still didn't tell Yuka about Shizuko. It still really didn't seem like it mattered. We were roommates by then and not even very close roommates.

Yuka said she wanted to stay in LA. If she'd said she wanted to move with me I would've figured out how to take her. We could go somewhere else. Somewhere cheaper. But Yuka didn't want to go. I told her there was no point in continuing to live as a pair of marginally friendly roommates. One of us needed to make the decision to pull the plug on this thing, and I had made it.

There was never any anger in our exchanges. No. I take that back. I did get angry at her for a day. But that took too much energy, so I stopped it. No, our life together ended not with an enraged bang but with a softly voiced, dejected whimper.

So my mom was dead, my job was over, and it looked like my eight-year marriage was finished as well. I wasn't sure what had happened. Maybe it sounds strange to you that a Zen teacher wouldn't know. I don't blame you. When I first got into studying Zen I figured Zen teachers were all-knowing and all-seeing myself. Plenty of spiritual teachers — particularly in mystical Eastern traditions — like to pretend they *are* all-knowing and all-seeing.* But, alas, it doesn't work that way. I wish it did.

All I knew for certain was that changes needed to be made and they weren't going to be made by anyone but me. One of the diseases that befell Nakano Productions was the growing belief among the management that no decision should be undertaken unless there

---

* This is far less prevalent in Zen than in some styles of spiritual practice, though I have seen it with Zen teachers too, unfortunately.

was absolute certainty it would be successful. In my years of exposure to them that same belief had crept into my psychological makeup as well, even though I knew full well it was crap. You'll never work out all the angles. You just have to make the best decision you possibly can, given what you have to work with at a particular juncture in your life.

I knew my idea wasn't great. But it was the best I had. I'd have a chance to research it because I'd weaseled my way into a speaking engagement at McGill University in Montreal a few days after the upcoming gigs I had scheduled in New York. Montreal is only a short plane ride from Manhattan. My friend Thibault in Montreal was kind enough to set up the talk after I begged him to find me some excuse to go there. My publishers also got me a CBC radio noontime talk show with Anne Lagacé Dowson, one of the country's most popular hosts. Sweet. But before any of that I was on my way to New York City.

Although the three live gigs and two radio shows I did in NYC were very cool, the best was definitely my talk at the Interdependence Project. The Interdependence Project is a Buddhist-based grassroots nonprofit organization based in NYC's hipper-than-you'll-ever-be East Village. They've got a real good thing going there up in the third-story yoga studio they use for their talks. The place was packed to the rafters when I showed up. You'd think New Yorkers would have better things to do. What impressed me even more was that when I suggested we all do a bit of zazen before the talk began, nobody gagged or ran away. They sat good, although it was only ten lousy minutes. My talk was well received, and the questions were good.

A couple of fellow Ohioans showed up and took me to a good place for Vietnamese sandwiches afterward. Very nice of them. A guy named Marc Catapano from Renagade Nation TV — a business founded by Little Steven Van Zandt of Bruce Springsteen's band — was also at the talk. The next day he showed me around town, including a tour of the famous spots of Greenwich Village and his own very groovy office. It's always really nice when people do stuff like this. I travel alone to these out-of-town gigs. No roadies, no drummer to pal around with. So it's good to have somebody to talk to.

The following day I spoke at a bookshop in Greenwich Village. The Q&A was briefly hijacked by a couple of Christians who wanted to make some points of their own. That was a bit odd. I thought New Yorkers were all Jewish!*

The only downside of the New York City gig was the vicious killer cat I had to share an apartment with. Now, don't get me wrong. I am very grateful to the woman who let me stay at her swingin' NYC apartment for free while she was away. But man, oh, man, her cat was a total psycho. The first night it was just me and kitty. He attacked me twice without the slightest provocation. The first time he drew blood. The second time I ran away. I found I could deal with the daylight attacks by just keeping a safe distance. The trouble came at night when he'd station himself outside the bedroom door and growl and hiss at me when I tried to make my way to the toilet. Because I drink about 12,000 liters of water a day this is a frequent occurrence.

The first night I managed to chase him away long enough to get into the toilet. But then he waited outside the bathroom door ready to jump me when I came out. I grabbed a plunger and jousted at him to hold him at bay long enough to get back to bed. The plunger worked okay that night. But the second night some other houseguests showed up. They'd also been invited by the owner of the place and would be staying in the living room. Rather than risk waking them up with several noisy cat confrontations each night I resorted to peeing into an empty water bottle. From this experience I learned that I can pee out 500 ml of nearly crystal-clear piss over the course of a night. I think it's sposta be a good sign if your pee is pretty colorless.

---

* Just calm down, I'm kidding. Still, Greenwich Village is not exactly known as a hotbed of fundamentalist Christianity.

The third night I'd had enough of that. So I set up a barricade to keep the cat out of the area between the bedroom and the toilet. This would keep him away from his food dish for the night. But since it was already midnight when I got back to the place and I planned to leave for Montreal at 5 a.m., I figured kitty would survive the intervening hours without dying of starvation. However, my host's other houseguests arrived back at the place at about 1 a.m. They got very, very, very upset at the idea that kitty cat might be deprived of food for an entire night and called the host to complain. I was kicked out for my cruel abuse of the poor, sweet, darling, helpless little animal. Fortunately, the woman who'd set up my gig at the Interdependence Project lived down the hall and I was allowed to use her couch for the night.

Look. I like cats. I had a cat of my own named Shithead who cost me hundreds of dollars in vet's bills and special food, owing to repeated kidney infections at a time when I was making about $200 a month at shitty Dimentia 13 gigs and temp work for Kelly Services. When I moved into Tim McCarthy's Kent zendo there were five cats in the place among the various members of the house. I even get along with my friend Nina's cat Lilly, who is also famous for attacking visitors but who seems to love me.

But I made it through and did not get mauled by the fiendish feline. The things a traveling Zen master must deal with! It was onward to the Great White North!

## CHAPTER 25

# ALTERED STATES
# IN AN ISOLATION TANK

*W*hen I arrived at the Montreal airport I went straight to the house Shizuko shared with several other university students. She was glad to see me.* But as we sat together on the couch she said, "This is a dream for you, isn't it?"

I knew what she meant. For her, being in Montreal was part of her real, day-to-day existence. Me, I just flew in there, hung out for a few days, and zipped back off to my real life. I couldn't be a decent boyfriend to her. I was married, I traveled all the time, I lived several thousand miles away, and as much as I wanted to move to Montreal, the prospects of my doing so any time soon were pretty dim. We talked about it a lot and decided just to enjoy our time together without too much concern for where things were going to end up.

Thibault, the guy who got me the speaking gig in Montreal, is a grad student at McGill University's Counseling Psychology Department. He's interested in Zen as well as in the various technologically enhanced meditation methods now on the market, such as

---

* Or was that just a banana in her pocket?

sensory deprivation tanks and sound and light generators intended to induce meditative states. Because of his research work Thibault has access to a place where you can rent time on some of these machines. Knowing full well that I have said some not-so-nice things about such mechanical meditation devices in the past, Thibault invited me to come and check out some of them for myself.

At the outset, let me tell you that I don't believe sensory deprivation tanks and sound and light generators for meditation are bad, or evil, or any of that. But I will say very emphatically that the effects they produce have nothing to do with what we are aiming at in Buddhist practice. There is tremendous confusion on this issue, even among those who ought to know better. I once saw a Buddhist master tell his student that she could make years of progress along the Buddhist path by spending just a few hours in a sensory deprivation tank. He was full of shit. Then there are the ads you find in Buddhist magazines claiming that sound- and light-generating machines can have you meditating as deeply as a Zen monk in minutes with no prior experience. Also bullshit.

When I've said this before, certain people always go, "You've never tried these things! How can you possibly know?!" This is ridiculous logic. You don't always need to try something for yourself to know what it is. I'm certain, for example, that dog shit does not taste like chocolate without ever having done a blind taste test. In any case, now that I've tried the damn things none of those crumb-bums can ever again tell me not to knock 'em if I haven't tried 'em. So there.

And truth be told, I've always had an interest in sensory deprivation tanks. One of the first books I ever read about meditation was *Center of the Cyclone* by Dr. John Lilly. Lilly was a psychologist who was keenly interested in dolphins. He figured that if dolphins were as smart as people we should be able to communicate with them. Lilly was attracted to meditation as a way to plumb the inner depths of the mind to find the source of real communication and use it in his experiments with making friends with Flipper and pals. Since using them involves floating in saltwater, sensory deprivation tanks seemed to him the perfect way to get as deeply as possible into how the human mind really works and into what it's like to be a dolphin at the same time.

A sensory deprivation tank is like a really, really big bathtub filled with thick saltwater kept exactly at body temperature. The tub is enclosed on all sides by a fiberglass shell that shuts out as much sound and light as possible. You lie in this thing, shut the door, turn out the lights, and let the saltwater buoy you up so you never touch the sides and fill up your ears so you can't hear. Doing so, you lose almost all sensory information from the outside world.

Lilly used to like to enhance his sensory deprivation experiences with various psychedelic drugs. I've already had my fun with drugs — not!* Lilly thought he'd reverted back to his prehuman state during one such sensory deprivation tank acid trip. A highly fictionalized version of this story became the movie *Altered States*, wherein William Hurt plays a character loosely based on Lilly who goes into a sensory deprivation tank, takes some heavy-duty brain-altering chemicals, and emerges as a hairy ape-man who terrorizes the local college.

Much as I hoped I might turn into a hairy ape-man during my session, I figured it was probably pretty unlikely. Still, I was curious about what might happen. Apart from the ape-man bit, Lilly claimed to have had some profound life-changing experiences in these tanks, even without the use of drugs. Many others have made similar claims. Thibault told me that the last Zen monk he put in one of these said he hallucinated that he had left the tank and was surprised to find himself still inside.

---

\*  See my first book — ch-ching! It recounts a massively bad acid trip I had in my late teens that turned me off psychedelic drugs forever. Though I still dig the Beatles' *Revolver* album — an acid-inspired masterpiece.

In the movie William Hurt wears bathing trunks inside the tank. I guess they needed an R-rating. But the real world is rated NC-17, so I had to be stark naked. You gotta shower up before you get in too, to make sure you don't get any of your cooties in the water.

Once I got in I quickly discovered that I did not like the fact that my, um, bait and tackle bobbed out above the water like a little pornographic island. It's not like a normal bathtub where the bottom half of your body sinks. Still, I relaxed and tried to let the experience occur as it would. At first, in the absence of any visual evidence to the contrary, I experienced the tank as immensely huge, as if the ceiling were miles above and the saltwater extended to the edge of the known world. This soon passed when my feet bumped up against the edge of the tank. Still, it was a cool sensation for a couple of minutes.

To try and get as meditative as possible, as I lay there I attempted to establish the state of mind you get in zazen practice. I found this utterly impossible. Zazen is a physical practice and depends as much on bodily sensations and feedback — including a certain degree of discomfort — as any sport. The design of the sensory deprivation tank is based on the idea that mind and body are two distinct and eternally separate entities. The makers evidently figured that if they could effectively shut out all bodily sensation a person would experience the state of pure mind.

But the state of mind divorced from body never exists in nature. We imagine it could, but I've yet to meet or read about anyone who could persuade me they'd ever experienced such an absurd thing. But more than that, I find the idea absurd, given my own experience.

Close as it strives to come, the sensory deprivation tank didn't really provide the true sense of mind free from body. I could hear people walking around upstairs by the vibrations carried through the structure of the building. I could hear my own heartbeat. I could feel the water to some degree, and I was certainly aware of my, um, frank and beans flopping around there like a kielbasa carelessly thrown into the Great Salt Lake. I could also see darkness around me. And darkness isn't really the same as the absence of optical information.

In any case, I tried my best to let go. But after a few minutes I just nodded off. I was awakened at the end of my hour by some weird new age music that reminded me a bit of the soundtrack to *Voyage to the Planet of Prehistoric Women.*\* When I got out I was disoriented and dizzy. It took a minute or so to find my land legs again. This too was quite different from zazen, which has sometimes left me a bit stiff-legged but has never interfered with my natural sense of balance.

After I was done with the sensory deprivation tank, I got a chance to sample one of the sound and light meditation machines. According to the ads in the Buddhist mags, these are supposed to have you meditating as deeply as a Zen monk in mere minutes.

The one I tried was called the Pulsar. To use it you sit on a comfy fake leather recliner just like the one Dad used to slouch on to watch the Indians get beat by the Cubs. Then you slip on some DEVO-style sunglasses in which a bunch of little blue lights have been embedded. Finally, you strap on a pair of headphones and switch on the unit. A CD plays a series of tones that are synchronized to the lights embedded in the glasses so that the lights blink at different rates according to the tones. *Weeeeeee-woooooop-wahhhhhhhhhh-weeeeeee-woooooooop.* It sounds like outtakes from the theme song for *Doctor Who.*

While the sensory deprivation tank had been mostly relaxing

---

\* Famed schlock science fiction producer Roger Corman was on a trip through the Soviet Union after having been invited to a film festival in Yugoslavia and caught a screening of a Soviet educational science fiction film called *Planet of Storms.* He bought the US distribution rights, then called up twenty-seven-year-old newcomer director Peter Bogdanovich and told him the problem with the film was that there were no women in it. Corman told him, "Shoot women. We'll cut it in." Bogdanovich hired a bunch of hippie chicks, dressed them in bikinis made of seashells, and had them cavort around on the beach for a few days. To add a bit of name value, he cast fifties sexpot Mamie Van Doren in the role of the leader of the gill women. Bogdanovich cut the scenes of Mamie and the girls on the beach together with the Soviet footage and, voilà, Roger Corman now had something he could sell on the drive-in movie circuit. It's the best movie ever made. I'm not joking.

and pleasant, this thing was just annoying. But I was committed to giving it the old college try for the full thirty-minute dosage. After a while it stopped being annoying and started being boring, and once again I nodded off. I could not see the point of this one at all, I'm afraid. My only guess is that the tones might interrupt a person's train of thought and produce something that felt like whatever people who haven't got a clue in the world think zazen feels like.

So my verdict is that sensory deprivation tanks are pleasant enough and may have some therapeutic value but the sound and light machines are a complete waste of time. Both are highly artificial constructs. Nothing even remotely like either of them can be found anywhere in nature. They're intended to try and realize some idea that thought has created — the idea that the mind can be free from the body.

Zazen, on the other hand, is a very natural practice. You can do it anywhere at any time. It doesn't depend on any artificially imposed silence or synthetic noises and lights. In fact, artificial silence is detrimental to the practice. Although it's ideal to do Zen practice in a quiet place, there's no need to artificially enhance that quietude by trying to block out all sensory information. Zazen is also not based on achieving some goal created by thought. It aims to free us from everything that thought has constructed. This is a far more vital concern.

I stayed in Montreal a few more days after my talk, just checking out the city, wondering if I could live there. It seemed all right. Unlike LA, they have a viable public transit system, so I wouldn't need to be driving all the damned time. There was real weather out there. People were nice. I'd have to learn French in order to really appreciate the place. But this was a plus too, since I liked the challenge of learning a new language.

Shizuko and I talked a lot about this. She told me that the stuff I'd written about Yuka in my books had really moved her. She strongly encouraged me to go back and try to work things out. I was willing, but I didn't think it was going to work. Shizuko said she'd be my friend even if I moved up to Montreal with Yuka. And that if I moved there alone, we'd see what developed.

# CHAPTER 26

# *YOUR LIFE IS NOT YOUR OWN*

*A*fter rinsing off all that saltwater and kissing Shizuko good-bye, I left Montreal for Detroit to hang out for a couple of days at Still Point Zen Center, where I'd visited a few times before. Still Point is a Korean-style Zen place, although I've yet to see a single Korean person there. Their style is similar to Japanese Zen, but they do a whole lot of prostrations — 108 a day! It's like a workout! Vince Anila, the guy who runs the place, is a veteran of the '80s Detroit hardcore scene. Detroit was one of the places Zero Defex used to visit back in the day, so we have some stuff in common. Plus, he loves *Johnny Sokko's Flying Robot*, a very cool '60s Japanese monster TV show.

After a few days in Detroit it was on to Boulder, Colorado. My publishers had heard that Boulder was a hotbed of Buddhism, so they figured I'd have a good audience there and maybe sell a few books. They were so psyched about this they even paid my way out there.

While Boulder may very well be way into Buddhism, the Buddhism they're into in Boulder, generally speaking, is Tibetan Buddhism. Tibetan Buddhism is quite different from Zen. It's colorful, it's bright, it's full of rituals and chants. The Tibetans are the guys

with the prayer flags and the Dalai Lama and all the mandalas —
those groovy psychedelic pictures that look like big intricate circu-
lar patterns and stuff. Richard Gere's Buddhism is Tibetan. So is
Lisa Simpson's.

The reason the people in Boulder are so into Tibetan Buddhism
is because a Tibetan monk named Chögyam Trungpa started a Buddhist university called Naropa Institute out there. Trungpa was a bit
of a wild man. He was into what they called "crazy wisdom." I've
heard firsthand tales of him drinking three forty-ouncers of malt
liquor during a single one-hour dharma talk. He reportedly slept
with lots and lots of his students, made guests at his temple strip
naked at parties against their will, and generally caused havoc wherever he went. He died at age forty-eight allegedly owing to compli-
cations related to his alcoholism. According to his students, though,
he was a brilliant teacher of the dharma. And I have to admit his book
*Cutting Through Spiritual Materialism* is a favorite of mine. But I still
feel a bit of trepidation when I hear about his methods.

Be that as it may, the Buddhism they're into in Boulder isn't quite
the style of Buddhism I teach. I was really worried about how I might
go over in such a place. Would they run me out of town on a rail?
Would I get booed offstage? But my host, Waylon Lewis, the editor
of *Elephant* magazine, was gracious and generous. I had a real good
time. A guy named Kyle Larson showed me around his hometown of
Fort Collins and got me some gigs there as well. Cool.

Boulder is a place where people have long discussions with their
sushi chef about whether or not the mackerel and squid they serve has
been fished sustainably. I'm from Akron, Ohio, where the most likely
conversation with a sushi chef is, "Take this back, it's not even
cooked!" In other words, Boulder is a way more progressive town
than I'm used to.

While I was in Boulder at the sushi shop where people worry
about sustainable fish there was a guy outside on the street panhan-
dling. There are tons of panhandlers in Boulder, nearly all of them

young, white, healthy, and looking like the only thing they'll use your spare change on is recreational drugs. This particular white panhandler, not quite as young as most of them, had obviously used some heavy drugs in his past — perhaps even his immediate past — and put some serious wear and tear on his body. He was getting pretty belligerent with his companions, and I kept my eye on him to see if he started heading toward the restaurant's patio where I was sitting. Eventually he moved on somewhere down the street. Phew!

Watching that guy and my reaction to him I suddenly realized that my life isn't really my own. We all imagine that our lives and our bodies are our possessions. We figure as long as we don't do anything really egregious like knife our next-door neighbor or go shoot up the local grade school it's nobody's business what we do with ourselves. But I wonder if that's really true.

When that hobo was doing all his drugging and drinking and whatever else got him into the state he was in, he probably thought, "Fuck the rest of the world! *I'm* living *my* life the way *I* want!" Of course, I can't put words into his mouth. But I know that I have felt this way for most of my life. If I wanted to take acid it was my brain I was fucking with, and nobody had any right to tell me not to. If I wanted to stay out all night partying, I was the one who had to deal with the consequences the next day, so screw anybody who had any opinion about it. If I wanted to eat junk food instead of being healthy it was my body, and it was none of anyone else's concern.

But I'm starting to doubt that attitude.

Of course if you want to look or dress a certain way society has no business telling you not to. Just because someone doesn't like your tattoos doesn't mean you need to remove them. And just because someone doesn't like your Mohawk doesn't mean you need to get a Jay Leno–style blow-dried do. Your choice of a life partner is nobody else's beeswax either — except, of course, your life partner's. Making a decision about whether or not to terminate a pregnancy or vote Republican is a very personal matter, and no one else — especially employees of the federal government — needs to be consulted. It's also not your duty to keep everyone you meet satisfied. Most people are so thoroughly fucked they don't have the vaguest clue what they really need or even what they really want, and it's not your duty to provide them with what they *think* they want.

But having said all that — which is so obvious it's a shame it needs to even be stated — your life still isn't really just yours alone. This is why I don't do drugs. If I get high, I'm asking the rest of the world to take care of me. When I'm stoned I'm shirking my duties as a human being for the sake of a shallow thrill. If I don't keep my body in reasonable shape in general I'm also impinging on others. I take up more than my fair share of space on an airplane or bus. I get pissed off way too easily because my body never feels right so I can't think straight. If I get angry or otherwise overemotional, it's never just my own affair. I spread that anger to others through my careless actions. When you're angry you never, ever, ever act reasonably. Never. If I get depressed I force others to deal with my black moods. If I get distracted I might run over somebody's kitty cat.

This is why I do zazen. I discovered that when I didn't do it, my body and mind were too scrambled up for me to interact with anyone in a sensible way. It was through this practice that I began to see very clearly that I was not my own possession. I am a manifestation of the universe, duty bound to take full responsibility for everything I encounter. And everything I encounter is everything in the universe.

But there's another side to that. You're also just like me, an asshole. Seriously. A complete asshole. You have no idea what you are or what you're supposed to be doing. Yet you run all over creation like it's some cheap-ass toy Santa gave you that you're now gonna break, and then you cry until Santa gives you another one. 'Cuz there are a million of them all lined up on shelves at the store. There you are, out hooting and hollering your ugly head off at three in the morning and waking all the people on the street. Turning your moronic music up as loud as it can go to show the world who you really are. Racing your Harley down Sunset Boulevard at full speed. Dreaming of enlightenment you can buy in a box from some wind-bag Zen master and leave in your car while you go out and buy something else. Hanging out at tawdry meditation seminars hoping some genius guru will show you the Light, paying him good money for garbage fantasies. The universe is yours, and all you want to do with it is write your name in spray paint on the wall. You're like a dog pissing on a fence. No one who sees the mark you left on the world could give a shit. You're just exactly like me.

But sit quietly, and even a piece of gibbon's dung like you can see it. There's no one in the universe but you. You spread out all the way past the farthest galaxies, and that's just the beginning. Your thoughts are all stupid. Your perceptions are completely wrong. There's nowhere you can be but here. There's nothing you can know that's worth knowing. You have no future or past, and yet you'll always be here. And because of this you are God's eyes and ears on this world. You are God himself.

So pay a little attention, butt-wipe.

Sorry. Where was I? Oh. Boulder! That's it. The talks there went pretty well. I met some very cool people and took some very refreshing bicycle rides. I got all out of breath, though, from the altitude.

But the thing that happened in Boulder that most sticks in my memory isn't the talks and stuff. It's an email I got while I was there. It popped up in my in-box on the morning of September 11, of all days. It was very short and to the point.

Nakano Productions had just been sold.

# CHAPTER 27

## *SOLD! CHEAP!*

**N**ot only had Nakano Productions been sold; it had been sold for a sum so low that even a slacker like me could've gone to a bank and gotten a loan for that kind of money. I didn't have any inside info on how the entire company got bought for chump change. But I could guess.

I had no idea what the new management had in mind for me. But it hardly mattered, since I had no intention of continuing to work for Nakano Productions anyway. I arranged to go back to Tokyo for one last time to let the new management know where all the projects I was working on stood and to tell them that it would be up to them to take care of the rest.

The timing of all this coincided neatly with the annual Dogen Sangha zazen retreat. My plan was to get to Tokyo a few days before the retreat, go to the office, resign, and then focus my energy on the retreat. I made arrangements to stay in Tokyo with Ren Kuroda, a master swordsman and one of the regular participants in our retreats.

I'd be at his place for the first few days while I dealt with Nakano Productions and then on to the retreat. It was a watertight, infallible plan. Only it didn't work out at all.

Yuka decided not to go with me to Japan. In spite of the conversation we'd had after I returned from Great Sky, and all the rest, I still held out some faint hope we'd patch things up, at least enough to go to the retreat together.* Her not going with me really hurt. Not only emotionally but because she was always the one who could take care of the little administrative details of the retreats so I could be free to concentrate on being Mr. Zen Master for everyone. This was going to be a very hard trip. But if she didn't want to be with me I wasn't going to force her to.

The ten-hour plane trip was lonely, as was the long bus ride from the airport into town. But I was too jet-lagged to feel very sad. I decided that before I had it out directly with my bosses I'd better go say good-bye to Mr. Serizawa. Serizawa-san had been brought into Nakano Productions after he retired from a position at the Los Angeles office of one of Japan's biggest film studios. He was now a member of Nakano Productions' board of directors and was perhaps the only person in a management position at the company who ever made any sense at all. He was the only one with any real experience working in the film industry outside Nakano Productions. And he was the only one who ever paid attention to the opportunities I kept bringing in, though he was always voted down when he recommended them to the rest of the board.

I figured the Nakano family had sold the company out to the highest bidder they could find and that Mr. Serizawa was out on his ass just like I was. We'd become friends in the two years he'd worked

---

* I'm obviously not telling you everything that was said. In spite of what I'm trying to do in this book, there is still stuff I'm choosing to keep private. Okay?

there. My plan was to go meet him, drink a couple of orange juices while he drank a few beers, reminisce and commiserate a bit, then go to my meeting with the bosses the following day.

But when I met Mr. Serizawa he asked me if I knew the details of what had been happening with the company. I said I only knew what I'd seen on the Internet — nobody at the company ever gave me anything more than the most basic info. "Well, then, I'll tell you everything," he said. He explained to me the circumstances of the buyout, which I won't go into here. But because of those circumstances he would be staying with the company in a managerial position. He told me that he planned to get rid of both my current bosses but that he wanted to keep me.

Oops. That threw a bit of a kabob into the machinery. I still could have said, "Sorry, Mr. Serizawa. I've already decided to quit." But like a lot of Japanese businesspeople, he is very good at personalizing business. If I said no, it wouldn't just be turning down a job opportunity. I'd feel like I was letting down a friend. I said I'd consider it. He didn't have a concrete plan yet and seemed to want me to suggest something. But I had nothing to suggest. I had absolutely no ideas about my future at Nakano Productions. As far as I was concerned I didn't *have* any future at Nakano Productions. I went back to Ren's place and stared at the ceiling for a long, long time before I finally went to sleep.

The next day's meeting with my bosses was a total waste of time. But I still needed to go through with it anyway. I had to pretend like I hadn't heard any of the things I'd heard from Mr. Serizawa the previous evening, particularly the stuff about the two people I was meeting with getting fired and me staying on. In the past I might have worried about whether not revealing something like that was the same as lying. But they'd both find out soon enough. And in any case it was not my position to break that news, so saying anything about it would cause more harm than good. I got through the meeting by nodding a lot and listening to what they had to say, which ultimately wasn't a whole lot anyhow.

The next day I'd be starting a four-day zazen retreat. Once again I'd have plenty of stuff to think about while I tried to think the thought of not thinking and lead others along the path of enlightenment. Fun, fun.

# CHAPTER 28

## *RETREAT!*

**Y**uka's decision not to come along left me with some pretty hairy problems. In the past she'd been the one who pulled the retreats together. She placed the ad in the paper, kept records of who had signed up, called the futon rental place to be certain we'd all have stuff to sleep on, called the temple to reserve the space and the proper number of meals each day. She really did a lot. This time Ren and my friend Gerhard, who'd also been ordained by Nishijima, would handle that stuff. In the past I also had depended on Yuka to keep people doing what they were supposed to be doing when they were supposed to be doing it. As a shop manager she's good at that. I, on the other hand, am exceedingly poor at people management. Now I had no choice but to take charge of it myself. Ugh.

Ren woke me up bright and early the day we were set to leave for the retreat to say there was some kind of major problem with the water in his apartment. There was a huge puddle welling up from somewhere under the hallway carpet. The superintendent was called, and it was quickly discovered that one of the pipes somewhere under the floor had burst. This was a major disaster since there was no way to access any of the plumbing except to dig up all the floors. This project was gonna be pretty huge, and there was no way Ren was going to make it to the retreat, at least not the first day.

This was another major blow. With his background in Japanese sword fighting, Ren was exactly the kind of tough-guy type I needed to help do the stuff Yuka did to keep people in line.

It's a sad fact of life that even the kind of people who attend Zen retreats need to have someone who can keep them in line. In the Rinzai tradition they have a specific position called *jikijitsu* to handle this job. The *jikijitsu*'s role is to yell and scream at everyone who breaks the rules and hit them with a big ol' stick called a *kiyosaku* — which means "staff of instruction" — if they still don't get the message.*
The brilliant thing is that the position of *jikijitsu* rotates. The guy who's doing all the yelling and hitting one day is just a regular grunt the next, and someone else gets to scream and shout at him.

But the Soto tradition, of which Dogen Sangha is part, never adopted this system. Folks at Soto temples generally don't yell when rules are broken, and the "staff of instruction," if it's used at all, is usually only used on people who specifically ask for it. The person raises their hands in *gassho*, basically the same position as folding them in prayer, and the attendant comes along and whacks them on the back.

And why, you may wonder, would people ask to be hit with a stick? I told you zazen was really boring. It's also tough to stay alert during long periods of sitting practice. People who ask for the stick while sitting zazen say it wakes them up and stimulates the nervous system, something like a shot of espresso. Once someone asked Nishijima about this use of the big stick. After listening to a

---

* In contemporary Zen centers this stick is generally used in a very specific way during sitting practice. So it's not like the *jikijitsu* is roaming around the temple ready to wail on anyone who fails to bow properly or something.

long-winded explanation of the benefits of getting hit he finally said, "That's true. But I think it's more valuable to learn to wake up by yourself."

So we don't use the stick, and we don't have a *jikijitsu* to yell at everybody. I was on my own. Up Zen creek without a big stick.

This would be my fourth time leading the annual Dogen Sangha retreat. I prayed it wouldn't be as much of a disaster as the first time I led one of these retreats a few years earlier. Let me tell you about that! (Cue flashback music.)

Nishijima had been running these retreats several times a year for about twenty years when he decided he was too old and tired to do it anymore. I'd already taken over his weekly English-language lectures at the Tokyo University Young Buddhist's Association. So he asked me if I'd mind running the retreats for him too. What was I gonna say? No, you old coot, go run 'em yourself? Since that wasn't really an option I accepted.

I'm not by nature a confrontational, in-your-face kind of guy, I swear to God. At that first retreat I just wanted to be a laid-back, mellow Zen teacher, dispensing kind words out there in the beautiful temple with nice people enjoying a nice Zen retreat together.

Depending on whose standards you go by our retreats are either incredibly easy-breezy or gut-bustingly grueling and awful. They're certainly way easier than the Great Sky Sesshin. We get up each morning at 4:30 a.m. and do six periods of zazen a day with breaks for meals, lectures, work periods, and even a bit of free time for walks in the woods thrown in as a bonus. Whenever we hold our retreats one third of the people complain it's too hard, one third complain it's too easy, and the others just keep their opinions to themselves.

There are several buildings on the grounds of the temple we use besides the temple itself. One of these is a large guesthouse down the hill a bit from the temple itself. In previous years we'd always slept in a couple of rooms inside the temple proper. That year, though, they told us we could stay in the guesthouse.

While the rest of the attendees stayed in the guesthouse, I chose to stay by myself in the room above the kitchen at the temple proper. This is what Nishijima had always done. Having a room alone gave him a place to change in and out of his robes, to prepare for his lectures, and, most important, to hold private discussions with anyone who wanted personal instruction. I chose to follow his example. That was my first mistake.

While I was up in my room, one of the residents of the temple — only the head of the temple is an actual monk, the others are laypeople — was showing the folks down at the guesthouse the lay of the land. At some point he told them, "Feel free to use the place as you like." This is a standard Japanese phrase that actually means something more like, "Don't fuck with my place, or there'll be hell to pay." Unfortunately the folks on my retreat were not Japanese, so they took what he said at face value.

I didn't know the extent to which they followed his advice until the retreat was over and I got home. About two days after I returned I got a call from the guy who had told our people to use the place freely. He was practically screaming down the phone at me, saying he would never allow anyone from Dogen Sangha to use their temple again, that we were the biggest bunch of rude, uncouth, irresponsible good-for-nothings he'd ever associated with. The tirade went on for several minutes until I finally managed to calm him down enough to tell me what had happened.

It seems he'd left a bunch of plastic bottles of some kind of soft drink in the fridge. During one of the breaks, our guys had scarfed them all. Not only were these his drinks, he said, but he was apparently on some kind of medication and had mixed his medicine into several of these bottles. Don't ask me why. So our guys had drunk up not only all his refreshments but all his medicine as well. I never did find out what kind of medicine it was. But I didn't get any reports of people hallucinating or having sudden, urgent bowel movements. So it must not have been anything really strong.

I apologized profusely, then called up Nishijima to tell him what happened. He recommended I travel back to the temple and apologize in person, bringing the customary apology gift. I'd already taken some days off work just to run the retreat, so I was pretty busy when I came home.* The trip down to Shizuoka took three hours each way and cost about $120. But it had to be done, so I bit the bullet and did it. I even dressed in a suit and tie in that beastly hot late-summer weather to make a stronger impression.

My apology was accepted, and we were allowed to use the temple again. But I was still totally dumbfounded by the whole incident. Why on earth would anyone think that they could raid the refrigerator at a Zen retreat? The only possible reason, I decided, was that my attitude had been too lax. Everyone had looked at me being all free and easy and decided they could be free and easy too. This would stop. I'm not good at being a hard-ass, but I have been doing my best at retreat time since then.

At this year's retreat, with Yuka and Ren both gone, I decided the only way to make things work was to be even more of a hard-ass about stuff than I usually am. So I arrived at Tokyo station to meet everyone for the two-hour bullet train trip out to where the temple was with a chip on my shoulder and a big ol' can of bad attitude. Not really. But I was trying my best to be as much of a drill sergeant as I could in the absence of my goon squad of Yuka and Ren. Which really means I was a bit less of a wimp than I usually am.

This year's group was a pretty interesting mix. Several people who'd come in the past had signed up for the retreat again. Gluttons for punishment, I guess. But about half the people were newbies.

One of the newbies — let's call him Bucko, since I can't remember his name anyway, and I wouldn't want to embarrass him even if I could remember it — had a particularly resistant attitude toward the

---

* This was a few years before the situation with Nakano Productions had become a shambles, so I was actually *working* for them then.

practice. He'd done zazen with another teacher who encourages his followers to contemplate their breathing while sitting. "Breathing in, I breathe the thought of compassion, breathing out, I breathe the thought of a triple-decker burger with all the trimmings." Or some such thing. He asked if he could do that at our retreat.

I'm not really sure why he felt he needed my permission. No one was going to look into his brain and see what thoughts he was having while doing zazen. Rather than as a request for permission I took his question as an opportunity to explain our attitude toward that kind of practice.

In the book *Eihei Koroku*, Dogen addresses the issue of these kinds of breath-related thought exercises:

> In our zazen, it is of primary importance to sit in the correct posture. Then, regulate the breathing and calm down. In Hinayana,* there are two elementary ways [of beginner's practice]: one is to count the breaths, and the other is to contemplate the impurity [of the body]. In other words, a practitioner of Hinayana regulates his breathing by counting the breaths. The practice of the buddha-ancestors, however, is completely different from the way of Hinayana. An ancestral teacher has said, "It is better to have the mind of a wily fox than to follow the way of Hinayana self-control."
>
> There is also the Mahayana way of regulating breathing. That is, knowing that a long breath is long and that a short one is short. The breath reaches the *tanden*** and leaves from there. Although the exhalation and inhalation are different, they both pass through the *tanden*. When you breathe abdominally, it is easy to become aware of the transience [of life], and to harmonize the mind.

---

\* Hinayana is a derogatory term for the older forms of Buddhism that existed before Zen and are still practiced today. The Zen tradition is part of a later development called Mahayana, or "great vehicle." Hinayana means "puny, girly-man vehicle."
\** Tanden is that spot in the lower chest where the breathing muscles are.

My late teacher Tendo said, "The inhaled breath reaches the *tanden*; however, it is not that this breath comes from somewhere. For that reason, it is neither short nor long. The exhaled breath leaves from the *tanden*; however, it is not possible to say where this breath goes. For that reason, it is neither long nor short." My teacher explained it in that way, and if someone were to ask me how to harmonize one's breathing, I would reply in this way: although it is not Mahayana, it is different from Hinayana; though it is not Hinayana, it is different from Mahayana. And if questioned further regarding what it is ultimately, I would respond that inhaling or exhaling are neither long nor short.

My take on this is that Dogen was obviously not down with the whole counting the breath thing and certainly would not have gone for the whole "breathing in I think of flowers, breathing out I think of kittens" thing. But he wasn't completely negative about a bit of mild fixation on the breath as a means of settling the body and mind down during practice.

The idea that we can "breathe in the thought of compassion" or whatever sounds real nice. But there's a huge difference between real, honest compassion and the thought of compassion. The latter is ultimately just another kind of thought. Real compassion is vital to Buddhist practice. But it doesn't come from thought. It comes from intuition. Dogen said that true compassion is like a hand reaching for a pillow in the night. Compassion is spontaneous action that produces benefit to others and to oneself. Like the hand reaching for the pillow in the night, when true compassionate action is performed there is no sense of doer, and nothing even seems to have been done. And yet the world emerges improved for that activity.

Bucko didn't like my answer, nor did he like it when he asked permission to sit in a different posture from the rest of the group and I told him I would prefer he did not.

Ultimately Bucko found the retreat too difficult and ran away sometime during the second day without telling any of the organizers. This caused us some problems. Things that he'd been assigned to do didn't get done, and other members of the group had to pick up the slack. Not a disaster. But it interrupted the flow of the retreat in an unnecessary way.

Look, everybody. A Zen retreat is not a visit to Disneyland or Club Med. You are not a customer or a guest. It is not the job of those who manage the retreat — including the teacher — to cater to you. You are an active participant who is expected to work with the rest of the group to make the retreat happen. Leaving without notice is like deserting your job without notice. Everyone else has to do the work you agreed to do, and that's a problem.

This kind of stuff happens at all kinds of retreats all the time. I don't know why so many people fail to do any research before signing up for a Zen retreat. You, dear reader, are researching it right now just by reading this book. Good for you. Every time someone gets disgruntled about our retreats it's because they don't have the vaguest clue what to expect. It's perfectly normal to want to run away from a Zen retreat. I have these thoughts at every single retreat I attend, and I expect to have them up till the final retreat I ever go to. It's even okay to run away if you really feel you must. But tell somebody! Don't just skip out. By attending a Zen retreat you are accepting a position of responsibility. Honor that responsibility.

In any case, once Bucko was out of the picture, the rest of us got down to some serious Zen business. Ren's landlord moved his family to a hotel, so he finally made it to the retreat. I'd almost forgotten that Ren wanted me to give him the Buddhist precepts during the retreat in the kind of big-deal formal ceremony that I basically hate. That was gonna be fun.

## CHAPTER 29

# TAKING AND GIVING THE PRECEPTS

**M**y friend Norman — the guy who directed that documentary about Godzilla — told me a funny story about how he almost joined the army. Norman is a skinny, unassuming red-haired Woody Allen–type guy. He's been living in Japan for something like fourteen years making his living covering Godzilla movies as the correspondent for one of America's best-known horror film rag-o-zines, *Fangoria.*

Many years ago when he was in his twenties and still living in the States, he found himself down on his luck. He'd heard that guys with college degrees could get easy assignments in the army, so he went through the recruiting process. At the very last minute he made up his mind that he would not join after all. But by the time he had made the decision he was already in the waiting room with all the guys who were there to swear their loyalty oaths and officially become members of America's fighting forces.

The atmosphere in the room was pretty noisy and rambunctious. After all, you've got a bunch of guys in their late teens and early twenties who are preparing to take on a job whose main selling point is that you get to blow stuff up. At some point a big ol' drill sergeant guy steps quietly into the room. He goes around table by table saying in a meek, mild voice, "Excuse me gentlemen, it's time to go take the oath. If you wouldn't mind stepping into the other room." He's all soft and sweet, all "pardon me," "excuse me," and "please."

When he gets to Norman he says, "Sir, I'm sorry to bother you, but would you step into the other room for a moment, if you don't mind." Norman told him he'd reconsidered and decided not to take the oath. If the drill sergeant was taken aback by this he didn't show it. He just said, "Oh, that's quite all right, sir" and continued rounding up the other guys.

Pretty soon Norman was alone, waiting for the rest of the group to come back out. He could faintly hear them swearing allegiance to the United States Armed Forces down the hall. After a bit they returned and continued carrying on, laughing, slapping each other's backs, and all the rest.

The drill sergeant stepped back into the room, looked around, then bellowed as loud as a charging rhino in his roughest, gruffest drill sergeant voice, "Shut the fuck up!" The guys in the room were shocked into quiet. The drill sergeant pounded a fist into his hand, smiled, and said, "We've got you now." Norman says he never saw so many faces drained of blood in his life.

Which goes to show you that vows are serious business in the human community. When someone swears they're going to do something, we take that as binding. Even our legal system recognizes the validity of spoken oaths.

Buddha knew the power of taking vows and used it as a way to bind together people interested in pursuing the truth. The first vows required by Buddhist monks were dirt simple. When someone asked Buddha if he could become a monk Buddha just answered, "Welcome, monk!" Easy-peazy.

But it didn't take long for rules to develop in the Buddhist community. Someone would do something asinine, his friends would ask

Buddha if that was cool or not, Buddha would say that it wasn't, and a rule would be added to the roster. By the time Buddha died there were hundreds of these rules. On his deathbed Buddha said it was important to keep the major rules but that the minor ones could be ignored. Buddhists have been arguing ever since about which rules were major and which were minor.

I was looking at my copy of the *Vinaya*, the book in which these ancient rules were recorded, the other day, and some of the rules in there amazed me. I mean, come on. These guys needed *Buddha* to tell them not to trim their fingernails by chewing them all the way to the bone? They needed *Buddha* to tell them what to eat when they got gas? They needed *Buddha* to tell them it's okay to run up a tree if an elephant is chasing you? I swear to God, I'm not making these up.* Suffice it to say, there are a lot of *very* minor rules in the *Vinaya*.

These days a variety of ceremonies have developed in Buddhist communities all over the world in which folks who are interested in Buddhism vow to uphold the precepts — the rules they figure Buddha considered the major ones. Depending on which group you take the ceremony with, the rules themselves may vary somewhat. Also, depending on the group you join, once you've taken these vows you may be considered a monk,** or you may be considered a layperson who has taken the monk's vows.

Nishijima doesn't believe in making distinctions between monks and laypeople. So anyone who takes the vows is, to him, a monk. In the words of the great sixties punk band the Monks, "I'm a monk! You're a monk! We're all monks!"

I already wrote in my first book about my own experience

---

\* The elephant-chasing-you one is my favorite. If you don't believe me, check page 149 of volume 3 of the Sacred Books of the East edition of the *Vinaya* translated from the Pali by T. W. Rhys Davids and Hermann Oldenberg. The other examples I've cited are in the same volume, plus lots more.

\*\* Again, the way I'm using the word, monks may be male or female. I've never really liked the word *nun* a whole lot.

taking the Buddhist precepts,* so I won't repeat that here. When I got my Dharma Transmission certificate I became officially entitled to perform precepts ceremonies for anyone who wanted to take those same vows themselves. But, as you've probably figured out, I'm not real big on ceremonies to begin with, so in all the time that's passed since I became empowered to do it, I'd never given anyone the precepts. I know some guys who run right out and start giving the precepts to everyone they meet as soon as they can. Which is fine. But it's not my idea of a good time.

But Ren really, really wanted to receive the precepts. Lots of people really get off on taking the precepts. I was not one of those people. But then I'm not really a group joiner.

I do see the value of taking the vows. It's not like taking the oath to join the army — no one's gonna say, "We got you now!" after the ceremony is done. But it is a promise you make in front of a bunch of people. That makes it pretty hard to back out of.

The precepts we take in Dogen Sangha are as follows:

1. Don't destroy life.
2. Don't steal.
3. Don't desire too much.
4. Don't lie.
5. Don't live by selling liquor.
6. Don't discuss the failures of Buddhist monks and of lay-people.
7. Don't praise yourself or berate others.
8. Don't begrudge the sharing of the Buddhist teachings and other things.
9. Don't become angry.
10. Don't abuse the three supreme values: Buddha, the Awakened one; Dharma, the true teachings; and Sangha, the community of Buddhists.

---

* *Hardcore Zen*, available in fine bookshops everywhere. Ch-ching!

There's some good stuff about what it means to take these vows in a little pamphlet Nishijima wrote called *The Buddhist Precepts*:

Q: If we're afraid we won't be able to keep the precepts, what should we do? Does that mean we can't become Buddhists?

A: To answer your question we should consider the intent or purpose of the precepts. In most religions, precepts are considered to be commandments or laws of God. They form the basis of the religion itself and they must be adhered to strictly. But in Buddhism the precepts are fundamentally different. Keeping the precepts is not the aim of Buddhist life. Perhaps this sounds strange to you but it is the fact in Buddhism. Master Dogen said that following the precepts is only the custom of Buddhists; it is not their aim. He felt that the precepts were only standards by which to judge our behavior. As such they are very useful to us, but we should be careful not to make them the aim of our life.

The precepts have been described as a fence that surrounds a very wide, beautiful meadow. We are the cows in that meadow. As long as we stay within the fence our life is safe and serene and we can play freely in the meadow. But when we step outside the fence we find ourselves on shaky ground. We have entered a dangerous situation and we should return to the pasture. When we do, our life becomes safe and manageable again.

So to return to your question, as Buddhists we realize that in our long life there will be many situations in which we will be unable to keep the precepts. This should not prevent us from receiving the precepts. We receive the precepts sincerely, recognizing their value and purpose in our life. We esteem the precepts but we don't worry about them. This is Master Dogen's theory. It is our way.

Q: You mentioned that the moral code of most religions is based on the word of God. What is the basis of the Buddhist moral code?

A: The basis of Buddhist morality is reality itself. It is the order of the Universe itself. It is the facts of life, which are facing us at every moment. In Buddhist theory the most important thing to see is what there is. Buddhist morality is here.

In other words, Buddhist morality has no basis other than Buddhist morality itself. To understand this point we must realize that morality is not a theoretical or intellectual problem. Morality is a practical problem — a real problem. What to do here and now is the problem and the answer is contained in the situation itself. This is the fact, and facts are the basis of Buddhist morality itself.

Q: So what is the relationship between the precepts and morality?

A: The precepts guide us in our life. They have come from the experience of the truth in the past, so we can say they are based on reality. But our lives are tremendously complex and varied. If we try to apply the precepts too strictly we may lose the freedom to act. We are living here and now so we must find rules that can be used here and now. We must find our precepts every moment. Reality is changeable so our rules must also be changeable. True rules must work in the real world. True precepts are changeable and at the same time unchangeable. This is the nature of Buddhist precepts. They help us live correctly. They provide a framework which is exact and rather narrow. And yet we are free to act in the moment by moment situation of our life.

A Chinese priest once said, "No rule is our rule." This statement expresses the Buddhist attitude precisely. The precepts are valuable to us. They can help us before and after we act. But in the moment of the present we cannot rely on any rule. We must make our decisions directly. At the moment of the present to be without precepts is our precept. No rule is our rule.

Q: So is it important to keep the precepts or not?

A: It is important to keep the precepts.

So even though we can't possibly uphold the precepts, we vow to do so anyhow. Each time we break one, we need to do what's necessary to set straight all the stuff we knocked over and go back to upholding the precepts again. There may be times when people have to break the precepts to maintain true Buddhist practice. But those times are very, very rare. So it's always best to keep them as well as we can.*

But when I was upstairs at the temple putting on my robes and getting ready for Ren's big Buddha party, it wasn't the deeper meaning of the precepts I was worried about, or even my ability to keep them. I was more worried about whether I could pull off the ceremony. Not only had I never done a precepts ceremony before, but I would be doing this one in a real Zen temple, where it was entirely possible real Zen monks might even be watching. Japanese temple monks are notorious hard-asses about every goddamned little detail of their ceremonies. After all, they've devoted their lives to performing each step just right for paying customers. And I don't even know how to tie my robes up the correct way, let alone perform an official Buddhist ceremony.

Luckily for me, though, the only monk who stays there full-time is the master of the place, and he went out early in the morning the day the ceremony was to be held. With him out of sight the only guy associated with the place was the temple cook, who was not a monk.

Even though I'd read over the ceremony a bunch of times in the plane on the way over to Japan, and even though I'd gone through two precepts ceremonies myself — one in Nishijima's group and one with the official Soto school of Japan — there was no way I'd get through this thing without a script. But that was okay with Ren, since he'd need to follow along with the script as well. In the morning we went around the temple and scrounged up all the stuff we'd need to perform the ceremony: a sprig of pine, a bowl of water, an incense holder, a candle, a ceremonial chair, and a few other items. It was lucky we were in a place where all the necessary equipment was right at hand.

---

* Especially if you're me and you're all alone in Montreal for the night. We'll get back to that stuff later. Don't worry.

At the appointed hour I went upstairs and changed into my full robes. Well, more or less. As I said, it was beastly hot, so I went without one layer of the official underwear.* Nobody would see that anyway, and I hoped Buddha would forgive me. Though I knew if any real monks saw me dressed like that they'd chew my ass out for it.

I went downstairs, sweating already as I walked, and we got down to business. It went pretty smoothly. You have to do each vow three times, which is a pain in the ass and also boring. The only cockup happened when we got to the one that says, "Do not live by selling liquor." I sooooo wanted to say "Liquor? Didn't even *know* her" after each repeat of the vow, I could barely get through them. But I grimmed-up and made it to the end. By then I was sweating like a hippo in a sauna. We did our last bows, and I ran upstairs to tear the robes off and put on some shorts.

With that out of the way the rest of the retreat went pretty much like usual. No one died. No one was injured. No one drank any of the soft drinks in the fridge. All in all it was a very nice little retreat.

Now it was time to go back to Tokyo and face up to so-called real life again.**

---

\* There are two layers of white underwear-ish stuff involved in the proper robe.

\*\* A Buddhist retreat is very much "real life," by the way. I'm saying this ironically because so many people imagine a retreat as a kind of escape. Having said that, though, I have to admit that life on a retreat can be very different from life in the usual workaday world. And that's fine. Just remember, they're both equally real. In fact, life on a retreat is in many ways a bit closer to reality, if you ask me.

# CHAPTER 30

# MEANWHILE, BACK IN TOKYO

When I returned to Tokyo from my very first Zen retreat in Shizuoka over a decade ago, I remember being almost in shock. The lights, the cars, the crowds, the noise: it was almost too much to take. Each shouting shop owner, each screeching siren, each flashing neon sign was like Satan's fingernails on a giant chalkboard in my brain. Sights and sounds I'd taken for granted just a few days before seemed to claw at my eyes and ears, making me literally wince in pain. I felt like I'd stepped into the third tier of hell itself.

That feeling faded after a few days, and I got back into the rhythm of city life. But each year I went to another retreat, sometimes two or three, and each time I returned it was like getting hit in the face with a big dead fish. Sometime around my fifth or sixth retreat, though, I started noticing something even stranger.

I had thought there was a gigantic difference between the world I experienced at those Zen retreats and the world I experienced in my normal life. But with each retreat it was becoming clearer that it wasn't really the case. In fact, the two sides of my life were actually

very much the same. The thing that connected the two worlds was
me. I was not something apart from the places I inhabited. It wasn't
as if there was this eternally independent me who could be placed
into one situation or another. The quiet, restful mountains were me,
and screaming-mad Tokyo was me.

In understanding that, I found I was able to bring the retreats
with me when I left them. Life in a retreat is very disciplined. Every
move you make is clear. Even your interactions with people follow
a prescribed pattern. Life outside isn't like that. It's chaotic, scat-
tered, wild. But it doesn't have to be that way. Even if everything
around you is going bonkers, as long as you maintain your center, the
world maintains its center too. It's a funny thing. I'm not saying this
is easy to do. But before I'd sat a few retreats I didn't even imagine
it was possible. Knowing that it is possible, I find it a kind of obligation to do my best to maintain that outlook.* The world needs a center. I wish it had a better one than me. But if it has to be me, then I
have to do it.**

Returning from the 2007 retreat meant returning to the huge
mess that Nakano Productions had become. Then again, I'd returned
from Zen retreats to the messiness of Nakano Productions a couple
of dozen times before. It's always been a messy company. It was just
messier than usual.

When we got back to town I sat with Ren in the Starbucks in
Tokyo's disgustingly trendy Roppongi district, and he outlined a
business proposal that I could make to the company. It made perfect
sense. They would set up a company in America — a legit registered
corporation, not the half-assed liaison office thing I'd been doing.
That corporation would have two very specific goals: 1) to get a Zone
Robo movie into production in the US and 2) to get a legit, kick-ass
DVD release of the first Zone Robo TV show, which still has a huge

---

* Failing again and again and again...
** When I say "me" here, I, of course, mean "you" as well, dear reader.

cult following in America. I'd be pretty much on my own recognizance as to how I got those things done. None of this weekly-report micromanagement bullshit I'd been doing. He also told me I should ask for a percentage of the profits the US company made. It sounded good, so I wrote everything up and sent it off to Mr. Serizawa in an email.

Mr. Serizawa liked what he read and said he'd speak to the new management about it. But he wasn't the final decision maker, so there wasn't much he could tell me.

I was pretty much left hanging once again. But not really. On the one hand, no one is ever really on his or her own. We're social animals, so we do have to depend on other people. It's a common romantic dream to want to live completely free from other people. But it never really happens. You can meditate for nine years in your cave, but someone's still gotta bring you sandwiches.

On the other hand, when you get into a situation like this, working for the same company for over a decade knowing you're contributing something valuable even if nobody else notices, you can start to feel like your life is in their hands. It really isn't. People tend to get pretty panicky when their source of livelihood is threatened. But most of us do okay no matter what. I have a certain amount of blind faith that whatever I've put into the human community as a whole will be available to me as an individual, should I need it. I guess that sounds a bit starry-eyed. But I've seen it happen too often to have any serious doubts about the process.

Of course you don't get something for nothing. It's the effort that you put in that comes back to you in times of need. So you can't be half-assed and just expect to be rewarded for it. Now, I know some of you out there are probably reading this thinking I'm implying that anyone who's poor or homeless or what-have-you must therefore be a lazy good-for-nothing who deserves what he gets. But that's not what I'm saying at all. I can't speak for people in those situations because I'm not one of them. I'm only talking about what I've observed for myself.

I'd already decided to quit working for Nakano Productions. So the prospect of Mr. Serizawa refusing my offer and me not getting a job I'd only barely convinced myself I'd even be willing to do wasn't that devastating. I stayed in Tokyo for another week and had a couple more meetings with Mr. Serizawa. But nothing changed. I went back to Los Angeles.

## CHAPTER 31

# AKRON

**Y**uka picked me up at the airport. Nothing had really changed. During my stay in Japan we'd exchanged some emails about the stuff that was happening between us. The distance and the fact we were communicating by writing made certain things easier to say. But nothing got resolved. I returned to the same emotionally frozen apartment I'd left. I hated being there.* But I wouldn't be there long because I had to go to Akron almost as soon as I got back to LA.

My friend David Giffels, who used to play guitar for a band called the Difficult** that used to play with Zero Defex back in the day is now a writer for the *Akron Beacon Journal*. He's friends with

---

\* I'm using the phrase "emotionally frozen" to describe the situation because I can't come up with anything better. In Zen, though, we look on emotionalism as unnecessary. We all have feelings, and we all need to express those feelings. That's fine. But the word *emotion*, to me, generally means a feeling that's been carried too far. It's a feeling that the brain has latched onto and attached to the sense of self. This is too deep a topic for a footnote, I know. I wrote more about this in the chapter "Kill Your Anger" in my book *Sit Down and Shut Up*, available in fine bookstores everywhere.

\*\* They were called the Cult for a while. But when the English goth band the Cult started getting popular they became the Difficult.

Bob Ethington, formerly the drummer for the fantastic, Akron-based new-wave band Unit 5, whose song "Go Ahead and Kiss Her" should have been a monster hit. These days Bob books speakers to give talks at the Akron Public Library's spiffy new auditorium. Dave talked to Bob, Bob talked to me, and a date was booked for me to go talk to the people of Akron about Zen.

I was more nervous about speaking in Akron than I'd been about any other gig I'd done since I started doing these speaking gigs. It's one thing to talk about Zen in front of strangers who think you're a cool-guy author. It's quite another to talk about Zen in front of people who knew you as a ratty-haired guitar player who couldn't hold down a steady job.

Identity is a funny thing. We all think we have one. We have a driver's license to prove it! But in practice our identity changes all the time. Shunryu Suzuki said that when we do zazen we're just a swinging doorway, letting air in and letting air out. Joshu Sasaki said when we eat breakfast, we become a breakfast eater, when we take a shit, we become a shitter. In the Buddhist point of view it's not that we have a self and that self does various things. Our true self and the things we do are exactly the same. We are a function of the universe.

By the time the dust had settled with all my northeast Ohio bookings, I was scheduled to do a speaking gig in Akron on Wednesday; a Zero Defex gig in Akron that same night; another Zero Defex gig, along with a showing of my documentary on the Ohio punk scene, *Cleveland's Screaming,*[*] on Friday; yet another band gig at the Spitfire Saloon in Cleveland on Saturday; and a speaking gig at the Mansfield Zen Center on Monday. Just to make sure I wouldn't get bored during my downtime, we arranged for rehearsals and recording sessions for the band on the days that I didn't have a gig.[**] Oy!

---

[*]    Available now on DVD from Parts Unknown Records (www.partsunknownrecords.com). Get yours today!

[**]  The CD we made is available from CD Baby (www.cdbaby.com). Get a copy now!

Meanwhile, other developments were taking place. I was at Amoeba Records in Los Angeles when I got a call from my dad that my grandmother — the one who'd refused to see my mom when we came up to visit on the Zen Death Trip — had had a heart attack. The immediate prognosis was good. She was alive and in stable condition. But while she was in the hospital they also found some kind of blockage in her intestines. They were monitoring her to see if they'd be able to send her home. I called her. She sounded weak and tired, as you do after a heart attack when you're eighty-six. But otherwise she seemed pretty positive.

Dad and I worked out a plan whereby we'd arrive at Grandma's place more or less simultaneously about a week before my stuff in Akron was set to begin. I would spend the first and last parts of my time in Ohio with my grandmother near Cincinnati.* Pretty soon after her heart attack, the doctors sent her home. But they weren't sure how long she'd be able to make it. She could have as little as a couple months, or she might bounce back and live for a lot longer.

Grandma was still sharing a tiny house with my aunt, my cousin Tina, and Tina's seven-year-old autistic boy — the one who'd put her in the hospital with a broken hip a year or so before when he was tearing around the house and ran into her. This really was not the ideal place for an eighty-six-year-old woman recovering from a heart attack. But it was her choice to go back there, and that was that.

I started getting a headache on the ride in to Grandma's place from the airport. The pain grew until by the time I set foot in the house I felt like Curly when Moe puts his head in a steel vise and screws it down tight. I tried to be sociable, but after a while the pain was just too much to bear. I went upstairs, turned off all the lights, and just lay there on the bed. After a while my aunt came up and

---

* Cincinnati is in southwest Ohio, and Akron is in northeast Ohio. It takes four or five hours to drive from one to the other. Don't say you never learned anything from one of my books!

asked if I wanted one of the super-strong painkillers they'd pre-scribed for Grandma. Normally I would have said no thanks and just endured it. But I was there to cheer my grandmother up, and all I was doing was being sick. So I accepted. But in spite of the drugs, the headache did not subside. There was nothing I could do for the remainder of the night but lie there in the dark and try to keep from vomiting.

The cause of the headache was stress. It was such a presence in that house you could almost feel it oozing out the door. My grandma was possibly dying, I was splitting up with my wife and had to fig-ure out how to either break it to everybody or skirt the issue, there was the whole deal that went down with my mom the last time I was here, there was the fact we were all cramped in way too small a space.

You may be wondering why, with all my Zen training, I would still feel this kind of tension. If you are, I understand. When I first started this meditation stuff I also believed that it would fix me so that I'd never feel a bad feeling ever, ever again. It doesn't work that way, I'm afraid.

The practice *does* make this kind of stuff easier. But no amount of enlightenment will eliminate all stress and tension from your life. We all have a certain amount of karma to get through, and nothing can change that. Things, once set into motion, need to play them-selves out. The best you can do is learn how to add as little new garbage to the pile as possible. But this in itself is a very significant thing.

There are no techniques for doing this. The only technique in Zen is learning how not to add to existing tension. Thoughts and feelings come up, and we usually latch onto them, think about them, and generate more thoughts and feelings. Learning not to do that helps the situation immensely. Each of us needs to find our own way to do this, which is why no competent Zen teacher will ever try to tell you how. Believe me, if I could I would. But I can't.

I made it through the first day, only to be awoken the next morning by Tina's little boy having a major tantrum. Listening to him stomp and holler I could only think, "I know exactly how you feel, kid." The following day he was in much better spirits, and as a result the whole house felt nicer. When I was alone with Grandma she asked me if I thought Grandpa was still with us. I said that I did. I do. He died in 2000, and he'll never return. He didn't reincarnate. He didn't fly up to heaven or descend to hell. He isn't inhabiting the dark corners of the house waiting to jump out at us and go, "Boo!" But he is still here.

You could say he lives on in our memories of him, or in the influence he had on our lives, or in the genetic material he passed down to us. All that would be true. But that doesn't quite get at it. He's still here in ways we can't ever express in words. The same thing that stared at the world out of my grandpa's eyes and wondered what the fuck it was all about stares at the world out of your eyes and out of mine.

Of course I didn't say all this to Grandma. It just didn't seem appropriate. She was worried about what would happen to her. She knew her prognosis wasn't good, though I don't think they actually told her the doctors thought she only had two months to live. In any case, it turned out they were way wrong in that assessment.

Grandma kept saying she loved me. I said it back. I'm not sure we felt exactly the same way, though. Or maybe we did. I loved her in spite of my anger over how she'd treated my mom and dad. Still, that anger kept any sentimental feelings I might have had at bay. She's Dad's mother, I thought, and she's dying. But I was there more for Dad than for her.

# CHAPTER 32

# ROOM 666

A few weeks earlier, I was sitting in my room after returning from the trip to Japan trying to order up some plane tickets to Ohio when Yuka came in and said, "Do you mind if I go to Ohio to see your show?"

I was pretty taken aback by this. In all the time I've been doing out-of-town speaking gigs Yuka has only joined me once. Since then she'd never expressed an interest in going along, even when the folks who invited me offered to pay her way as well. I told her I didn't mind if she went to Ohio with me, but that I didn't understand why she wanted to do it now. After all, we were pretty close to splitting up. What was the point? She said she wanted to see Zero Defex perform and thought she might not get another chance. Okay, I said. Because of her work schedule, she would only be able to come out for one day. I told her it would be an awfully expensive concert, but I didn't intend to stop her from coming, if that's what she really wanted to do. The truth was I found her request really moving, but I couldn't say so. I think she knew.

Yuka arrived in Ohio a couple of days after me. Our singer Jimi Imij's ex-girlfriend Spanky Butt Bitch, leader of the band Screaming Smoldering Butt Bitches, drove me to pick her up and took Yuka on a tour of some of Akron's famous sites, like the blimp hangar and the Rubber Bowl. Then we went to Kent, a few miles to the northeast, to visit my first Zen teacher, Tim McCarthy. Yuka was less interested in gabbing with Tim than I was, so she and Spanky went and did fun stuff in town while Tim and I talked. But before we could chat, Tim made me play out one of his favorite scenes from *Star Wars*.

ME: The circle is complete. When last we met, I was but a learner. Now I am a master.

TIM: Only a master of evil, Brad!

Then we had to pretend to have a light-saber fight, and I got to say, "Your powers are weak, old man." To which he replied, "You can't win, Brad. If you strike me down, I shall become more powerful than you can possibly imagine."

It was funnier in real life than it is on paper.

Rehearsal the next day went well. We pretty much picked up where we'd left off at the previous Zero Defex reunion show two years before. Jimi Imij looked healthier than he did the last time, possibly because he finally got himself a job and a place of his own to live. Mickey still refused to use a drum stool and instead stalked the kit like an enraged animal. Jeffro had all his parts down pat and — dare I say it — played them better than our original guitarist, Tommy Strange, ever did. And Tommy *wrote* most of those songs! It was hard keeping up with those guys, but I did. Tomorrow would be the test, though. Not only was it our first live show in two years, but I had to get through a speaking engagement prior to playing.

Tim drove me out to the Akron Public Library a couple of hours early, leaving me some time to pace around like a heifer waiting to be slaughtered. I wasn't nervous because I thought the audience would be unkind. In fact, I knew I could count on their support. Akron's pretty good about supporting its own. But I felt so incredibly pretentious to be talking about so-called spiritual stuff in front of friends who knew me when I was scrounging around for lousy bar gigs to try and pay the $60-a-month rent at some punk rock house.

Some time before the gig I'd bought some cookies and stuffed them into my book bag. When they introduced me the first thing I did was to hold up the package of cookies and tell the audience, "If you're good, after the talk there'll be cookies for everyone." That seemed to work.

My sense of intimidation kept me from going into some of the more interesting aspects of the practice during the talk. When I opened it up for questions, though, I realized that the other half of the audience — those who hadn't come just because they were friends of mine — had some pretty interesting things to ask. I'd never realized there was any market for Buddhism in northeast Ohio. When I lived there, there sure as hell wasn't. But things had changed in thirteen years.

They were good boys and girls, so when we were done I handed out the cookies.

Next up on the agenda was Zero Defex's first gig in two years — and that one had been our first in twenty years. We were booked to play at a little bar called the Matinee in the Highland Square district. Highland Square is what passes for the hipster area of Akron. Two blocks of bars and cool clothing shops and an independent record store.

The band was smokin' — a lean, mean hardcore machine. Yuka was right up front the entire time we played. She's a brave woman. Up front at a Zero Defex show can be a very dangerous place to be. The bar was jam-packed. But there wasn't too much moshing, mostly because there wasn't enough room to flail around in that tiny space, and also because the old punk rockers in attendance didn't have the energy for that anymore. But it wasn't just old punkers in the crowd. At least half the audience was people who'd been in diapers when Zero Defex was thrashing around town the first time. Cool.

I played my butt off for Yuka. It was such a touching thing she did, coming all that way and spending all that money just to see us play. I couldn't let her down.

After the show we went back to the big fluffy bed at Mickey's house. (We stayed in Room 666.) But although there was no animosity between us, there was no fire either. Part of me wished we could have fallen in love all over again that night and made a nice little happy ending for this book. But it wasn't to be.

# CHAPTER 33

# *TAKING AIM*

uka's plane left Akron at 6 p.m. the next evening. We said our good-byes like friends. It wasn't really sad. Just a little disappointing. In any case, I was too busy to get very sad.

The next day Zero Defex had yet another gig up in Cleveland. We slaughtered 'em. It was 4:00 a.m. by the time we got done unloading all our gear after returning to Akron from the show. When you're doing a Zen retreat you wake up at 4:30 a.m., and the contrast between the two lifestyles hit me like a whack in the head from the big ol' cinder block Mickey uses to keep his drum kit from sliding around the stage.

I tend to downplay the issue of discipline in my writing about Buddhist practice, mainly because it seems like some people write about nothing but Buddhist discipline. But it's a very important part of the practice to live in a regulated, disciplined way. You can't expect to maintain a balanced body and mind if you're continuously going in eighteen different directions at once by staying out late, sleeping in till a million o'clock, getting drunk and stoned, chasing tail, and generally carousing. It just doesn't work.

But the Buddhist attitude isn't like the religious point of view on these things. Religious people tell you that you shouldn't do stuff like that because it's sinful and evil. Sin and evil don't enter into it. It's just a simple fact that if you want your brain and body to work the way they're meant to, you need to take good care of the machinery God gave you. No two ways about it.

At the same time, Buddhist practice isn't about being all austere and pure. Arbitrary designations of purity are useless. You know when your body and mind have been stretched and smashed and squeezed and pummeled just by paying attention to how you feel. And when I woke up way too fucking late the next morning with my head throbbing and half the hearing gone out of my right ear I knew I'd been pushing things too far. No guilt, no need for confession. I just needed to get back into balance.

Even with the late night, I managed to drag my ass out of bed and get to the weekly Sunday morning sittings Tim hosts at Kent State. The clarity of his talk reminded me that I ought to be doing more Buddhism and maybe a bit less rocking out. A guy there asked whether Buddhists worship Buddha. Tim answered, "You couldn't exist without the whole of the universe being just as it is, and the whole of the universe couldn't exist without you. So it's not really what you think of as worship. Instead, you have a sense of awe and reverence for the universe. But at the same time you know that the universe depends on you. So it's a mutually reciprocal feeling." This is something all of us can tune into any time we wish. But most of us miss it entirely.

The next day I had a Zen talk of my own to deliver. I'd been invited by the Mansfield Zen Center to give a talk on Buddhism at a tattoo parlor down there. Given my association with the tattooed cuties on Suicide Girls, it was an opportunity I couldn't refuse. That talk went a lot better than the one in Akron had.

Generally speaking, most folks in the US who are interested in Buddhism tend to be college-educated, white-collar intellectuals.

Mansfield is very much a blue-collar city where not too many residents have any use for college. It was a refreshing change but at the same time a bit of a shock. These people were not stupid, by any means. In fact, if you ask me, finding a way to avoid so-called higher education is a pretty smart move. Their questions afterward were very direct. The first one was, "What is Zen?" That is a great question. I wish more of the people I talked to wouldn't assume they knew the answer to that already. I sure as hell don't. I had a tough time with that one.

Just in purely historical terms, Zen was originally a reform movement created by Buddhists who thought that Buddhism had deviated too far from its roots as a form of meditative practice. But that doesn't really tell you what Zen is.

To me, Zen is a search for truth through action. It's less a religion or even a philosophy than it is an attitude. Vince Anila of Still Point Zen Center in Detroit sent me this nice story about Tim's teacher, Kobun Chino, that illustrates the Zen attitude pretty neatly: "As a master of Zen archery, Kobun was asked to teach a course at the Esalen Institute in Big Sur, California. The target was set up on a beautiful grassy area on the edge of a cliff overlooking the Pacific Ocean. Kobun took his bow, notched the arrow, took careful aim, and shot. The arrow sailed high over the target, went past the railing, beyond the cliff, only to plunge into the ocean far below. Kobun looked happily at the shocked students and shouted, 'Bull's-eye!'"

As I get deeper and deeper into it, I find that Zen is nothing at all like what I expected it to be. My arrow doesn't hit the nice little painted bull's-eye but goes exactly where it goes according to my real action. Life lands you in all kinds of funky-ass situations. You have to act out of where you really are, not out of some ideal of where you think you ought to be. That whole "ought to" business is just a waste of time anyway. It's never what it ought to be. You just can't do what you ought to do.

I'm sure a few people who read this book will write and tell me what I ought to be, or say, or do. I get a lot of that. I used to care. Sometimes, in spite of myself, I still do. Isn't that funny? Caring about what people think I ought to be, say, or do has never led to anything but misery.

But I do care deeply about taking aim.

My advice? Take aim carefully and let your arrow fly.

Wheeeeeeeeeeee!

## CHAPTER 34

# MEETING DEATH FACE-TO-FACE

*O*n Tuesday Dad called in a panic saying that my Aunt Sarah was saying that Grandma was dying *right now* and that he was running back to Fairfield this minute from Flagstaff, Arizona, where he'd been trying to drum up some business. On Wednesday Spanky Butt Bitch* was supposed to take me down to Columbus, where I'd catch a ride to Cincinnati with my friend Laura. I had no idea if I could revise my plans at this point.

Twenty minutes later I got another call from Dad saying that my cousin Tina had called him and said that Grandma *was* bad off, but not as close to death as Sarah was saying. Dad said he'd get to Cincinnati by Wednesday. I decided to stick to my original plan.

Wednesday morning I got a frantic call from Spanky saying she'd called the cops on her band-mate Cheeky Butt Bitch's boyfriend because he was at her door being belligerent. Now she had to take Cheeky out to Kent — about ten miles up the road in the wrong direction — to file charges against the guy. Oy vey!

---

* Zero Defex vocalist Jimi Imij's ex-girlfriend, as you'll recall.

All this kept us in Akron till about noon. With the change in drivers and everything else I didn't end up arriving in Cincinnati till around 7:30 p.m.

By then Grandma was in her bedroom with 24/7 hospice-care people at her side. I called my sister, but she was still too mad at Grandma to come, even knowing Grandma might be gone in a matter of days or even hours.*

When I poked my head into Grandma's room at first I assumed she was asleep because she seemed to be snoring. In fact, she wasn't snoring. She was gasping for breath and had been doing so for perhaps two or three days straight by then. When she did rest she'd just stop breathing altogether, sometimes for almost a minute. No wonder my aunt thought she was dying. Grandma slipped in and out of consciousness. If you yelled, she'd open her eyes and respond to you, although she couldn't talk. She didn't seem to be in pain. But who could tell? She would smile, purse her lips for kisses, and even attempt to give us hugs, though she could barely lift her arms. I got the impression she wanted to talk but couldn't get anything out.

I stayed in her room for maybe an hour and a half, then visited on and off for the remainder of the evening. It seemed like she needed rest, and I didn't want to keep forcing her to wake up. I went to bed at around 2:00 a.m.

At about 3:30 a.m. I was awakened by my Aunt Sarah saying, "Do you have any religious ceremony you want to do?" I had trouble processing this seemingly random question. Something must be up, I figured, and that's all that mattered. I shook off my hour or so of shallow, troubled sleep, gathered up the little book of sutras I always keep in my bag, and went downstairs.

Grandma's breathing was noticeably different from how it'd

---

* Here's something kind of odd — and take this however you like. The hospice woman assigned to take care of Grandma that night was named Stacey, like my sister. And her husband's name? Brad.

been the previous night. She was still gasping but much harder now, and she didn't take any rests. Me, Dad, Sarah, and Tina, plus Stacey, the hospice lady, all gathered around the bed. We all spoke to Grandma, though it wasn't clear whether she could hear us. I quietly chanted the Heart Sutra for her. Occasionally she seemed to respond to us. But it was hard to tell. Tina woke her son and had him say, "Good-bye, Grandma" to her. I'm not sure he really got it. Probably not. But given how his behavior had been the previous few days, I was amazed at how grown-up he was being about the whole thing.

After about an hour, Dad and Tina left Grandma's room. I stayed with Sarah, who was trying to ease Grandma into death, telling her that soon she'd be with Grandpa and Bob, Sarah's late husband, and trying to make it all sound very beautiful.

To say that my feelings at that moment were complex would be a massive understatement. I loved my grandmother. But she'd been so mean to my mother a few months back and she didn't seem to have any clue why that made my dad and my sister so angry at her. While I wasn't angry at the moment, I couldn't say I was precisely sad. She was dying. That was what was happening. Nothing more.

My aunt had been there when her husband had died and when my grandpa had died. She knew what death looked like. Grandma's breathing changed again. A different rhythm. Less labored. More even. It was time. I asked the hospice lady to go get Dad and Tina and began softly chanting the Heart Sutra again.

When Tina and Dad entered the room, Grandma opened her eyes once more and seemed to try and raise her body. Then she just stopped struggling and slipped away. By the time I finished chanting the sutra she was gone.

When I go, I hope someone is chanting the Heart Sutra. They say it's helpful to hear it chanted as you die. I don't know. But I suspect it is. In any case the Heart Sutra means a lot to me, and I'd like to hear it one last time before I go.

We all stayed up for a while longer, kind of shell-shocked. We didn't speak or cry or do much of anything. The hospice lady made the necessary calls to get her body taken away and all that stuff. After a bit I went back to sleep. I don't know if that was a callous thing to do or not. But I couldn't hold my eyes open any longer, and I was out like a light within seconds. By the time I woke up a couple of hours later, they'd taken her away.

I'd just witnessed my first death. It didn't seem horrible or frightening. I wish I could tell you something profound about it. But I can't. It was just like a thing that happens.

The following day, Friday, was spent mostly getting stuff together for the funeral, which was to be held on Saturday. I'm always amazed at how quickly funerals are arranged. We went through Grandma's photo boxes and put together a few boards of photos for display at the funeral. Then me, Dad, Sarah, and my cousin Rob, who flew in from New York, went and talked to the local Methodist pastor, a nice woman named Valerie, about Grandma so she could get her stuff together for the eulogy.

The funeral was Saturday morning at noon, at the same place my grandpa had his. I didn't recognize most of the people who showed up. Grandma looked pretty good. But my cousin pointed out that they had a red light shining right on her face to try and make her look more lifelike. Funeral parlors are pretty clever. I'm not a big one for open-casket funerals. I understand the purpose they serve, and maybe it works. But I knew she was dead without having to look at her all embalmed like that.

After the eulogy, the pastor asked if those in attendance wanted to say anything. Dad came up front and told the story about the night he and Grandma heard a noise in the house. They went up and got the family gun then stood at the end of Grandpa's bed arguing over who was going to wake him up. My grandpa awoke to see his wife and son holding a gun and saying, "You do it," "No, you do it." Grandpa said, "Don't anybody do it!"

The story got a laugh, which is always a good thing at a funeral.

Later at the cemetery the pastor did the standard funeral stuff
— "ashes to ashes" and all that. I chanted the Heart Sutra again, quietly by the coffin. Then we all went to a place called Rafferty's for
food. Not much there for a vegetarian like me. But I managed to get
a few side dishes together as a meal. It seemed like I'd been eating
nothing but fried crap for two weeks — French fries are vegetarian
food! I must have gained twenty pounds.

I was probably the only family member at the funeral who didn't
cry at some point in the proceedings. I just didn't feel moved to. Zen
training tends to make a person less emotionally charged in general.
But I had cried about Mom dying, even though I knew it was for the
best. I never felt moved to cry for Grandma. Not that I won't miss
her or that I didn't love her. But too much shit had gone down for me
to be able to just break down and bawl over her passing.

## CHAPTER 35

# IN WHICH I VOW TO BE AN ASSHOLE FOREVER

*I* returned to Los Angeles in a daze. You can't get more in touch with mortality than watching someone you love die. I thought I was pretty in touch with my own inevitable death before. After all, I'd embarked on the path of Buddhism because of the fear that arose in my teenage years when my aunts began to wither and die from a disease that might very well have been coursing through my own blood even then, just waiting to strike.

But watching my grandmother take her last breath with those blue eyes wide open as if appealing to someone to make it better really slammed home what death is in a big way. As the days passed the impact became stronger. I was going to be just as dead as her, and it wouldn't be long — even if I got another forty or even fifty more years. At the end of it all I'd be just as dead as my dead grandma. Just as dead as my dead mom. Just as dead as my dead aunts. Just as dead as my dead friend Iggy who hanged himself in 1983. Just as dead as Keith Moon and John Entwistle and John Lennon and d. Boon and Sid Vicious and Kobun Chino and Dogen and Buddha. Dead, dead, dead. Gone forever.

And I made a vow.

For the sake of my dead mom and grandma and all those other dead people, I vowed to be an asshole for the rest of my life.

What I mean by that is that I just don't give a shit anymore. I'm gonna pretty much say and do whatever I want from now on. This book is a manifestation of that attitude. If my mom and grandma hadn't died, if my wife hadn't left me, and if I hadn't lost my job, you wouldn't be reading this. Oh, I'd still have written a book. But it would have been a much milder piece of work than this one. Maybe a little commentary on some sutra or suchlike, but not the big snarly ball of confessional vomit you've been sitting through for the past several weeks.*

Of course there are limits to how much of an asshole I'll be. I'm not gonna go out and rape, pillage, and plunder. I'm not gonna be like a drugged-out hedonist or nothin'. But I'm not gonna pull punches with people anymore. I'm gonna say what needs saying and do what needs doing, and if people don't like it, tough titty for them. That doesn't mean I'm gonna get up in people's faces and say, "I think you're ugly!" or anything like that. Like I said earlier, sometimes you don't need to say absolutely everything. There's no need to hurt people's feelings just so you can feel like you're being truthful. But I've always been far too shy and indirect about a lot of stuff. Now when something genuinely needs to be said or done, I'm no longer going to worry that maybe I shouldn't say or do it like I always have.

Still, I am a Buddhist. So I'm turning into an asshole with twenty-five years of Zen practice under my belt. This may make me a slightly different type of asshole from an asshole who hasn't done that stuff.

One of the things that gets lost in the way Zen is presented these days is that the whole idea of Zen in the beginning was to answer the question, How can we live a truly happy life? These days in

---

* Sorry about that.

America, Zen stuff always gets all caught up in religious ideas of righteousness and holy-ocity. Fuck that shit. Buddha didn't want to find something holy; he just wanted a life that wasn't a fucking drag all the time.

In India in Buddha's day, just like in ours, there were two basic ideas about how you can have a happy life. One camp said eat, drink, fuck, curse, and do whatever the hell you please, because the only real thing in this universe is matter. There's no God, there's no Eternal Reward, all that shit is bupkes, so do what makes you feel good right now. We in the West rarely hear about this side of Indian philosophical life. Maybe because it's not as pretty as the more spiritual side. But it's every bit as powerful in India as the side we always hear about. The side of Indian philosophy we always hear about held that the material world was an illusion, that the spirit was the only true reality, and that you should mortify the body in order to experience spiritual bliss. The material world, they said, was a big ol' turd, and the best you could hope for was to make a better place for yourself in the life hereafter.

Buddha tried both these approaches, but he wasn't satisfied with either. The eat, drink, and bed-down-with-Mary approach seemed to hold out the promise of pleasure and plenty, but it never really delivered. You got fat and hungover, and Mary gave you the clap.* So he checked out the spiritual stuff and found that you could get pretty blissed out with those practices, but that whenever you weren't getting some kind of spiritual high you felt like total shit because you hadn't taken care of your basic bodily needs. So he founded what he called the Middle Way.

The Middle Way was not some kind of spiritual path designed to make us all holy with shiny pink halos on our noggins. It was a way to live a life that wasn't a piece of shit. It was a way to find happiness and stability in an unhappy and unstable world. That's really all any

---

* Or vice versa, of course. It just sounds better the way I wrote it.

of us are looking for, when it comes down to it. The stability of the Middle Way comes in our practice of zazen, which is the actual physical and mental practice of stability and happiness. A bit of zazen in the morning and a bit in the evening radiates throughout the rest of the day and night and makes everything better. That's all there is to it.

Morality is an important part of finding real happiness because we are all interconnected. I can't be happy if I make the people around me miserable under the mistaken impression that their misery is not intimately connected with mine. So if I don't want to be miserable I need to behave morally toward everyone I encounter. In Buddhism behaving morally doesn't mean following some fixed code of conduct. It means being careful.

But another aspect of Buddhist morality is that you have to do your part. You're not here just for yourself. You're here for everyone and everything you encounter. Your role is to do and say the things that need to be done and said from your unique perspective. God is too far removed from the universe to see himself clearly without splitting himself into a bazillion eyes and ears that watch over all aspects of himself.* Whatever perspective you have is the most valuable thing in the universe. You need to be fully yourself. At the same time, you need to completely forget any idea you have about yourself. Or, if you can't forget it, at least ignore it, secure in the knowledge that whatever you think you are isn't what you really are.

Doing and saying what needs doing and saying has to be handled carefully. But being careful and being timid are two very different things. Lots of folks who confuse Buddhist morality with the religious variety think Buddhism is about being timid, that the phrase "do no harm" means standing quietly in the corner and keeping to yourself. That's not the Buddhist way.

Watching my grandma die, I realized we all have a limited time

---

* Dogen says something like this in a piece called "Kanon," which I talk about in my previous book, Sit Down and Shut Up, in stores everywhere. Ch-ching!

in this place to do what needs doing. Even if I get a good eighty-six years like she did, that still won't be enough time to get it all done. So I'd better get my ass in gear and at least do a few of the things I was put here to do before I bite the big one.

The best way of life is to live the way you want to. But living the life you really want to live is not the same as living the life you *think* you want to live. If you don't know the difference, you very well might be better off living the life everybody else thinks you should.

You often hear people rail against being born in a world they never made. That's delusion. You are a real manifestation of the continuous operation of the law of cause and effect. The world you live in is a world you made for yourself. The social rules and norms you chafe against were rules you put in place by yourself for yourself to follow.

Before you can live the life you truly want to live, you need to find out what you truly want. That takes patience. You need to look straight into your own mind and weed out your real desires from the false ones you've created out of thought. I only know of one way to do that, and you should have figured out by now what that is. Yep. You got it. Lots of zazen.

Of course, you never get completely clear of your false desires. Even Buddha himself couldn't manage that trick. Those wonderful "enlightened beings" who tell you they've achieved that rarified state are just con artists. But once you've sat for a couple of decades it starts to get a little easier.

Thanksgiving was coming up. It used to be fun to spend holidays with Yuka. Our first Thanksgiving in America we were still doing zazen classes on Thursday nights. We decided to hold class on Thanksgiving Day. Naturally no one showed up. So the two of us did a half an hour of zazen and set out looking for a place to have dinner. We tragically underestimated how hard it would be to find a restaurant that was open that evening. Even Burger King was closed. We ended up at a little Greek restaurant. It was charming and lovely, a treasured memory even now. But it was clear nothing like that was going to happen this year. Yuka was not interested in spending the holiday with me, and I didn't want to force it on her.

I'd recently set up a MySpace account on the advice of my agent, who thought it would be a great way to promote my books. I noticed that Leilani, the cute girl from my Zen class who I had such a crush on, had joined as one of my MySpace friends. So I wrote her a little note, just to say "hello" and tell her I was back in Los Angeles after a long time away. She told me they were having a Thanksgiving dinner at the co-op where she used to live and asked if I wanted to come. I accepted the invitation.

I didn't know any of the other residents, but Leilani kindly introduced me to them. It was a fun group of young people eking out an existence on the fringes of the entertainment industry. At one point I ended up sitting on a couch next to Leilani, just chatting. I talked to her a little about my mother's and grandmother's recent deaths, and she told me that she'd watched her father die of cancer when she was twelve. The experience had profoundly affected her outlook on life, even as my own more recent experience was profoundly affecting mine.

She was planning to take the bus home, but I wasn't going to be doing anything later except going back to my apartment. So I offered her a lift. She was living at her mom's house out in Torrance, which was about an hour's drive from where the party was being held. I didn't care. I liked being around her.

On the ride out to her mom's place I made up my mind I'd tell her how big a crush I had on her. It didn't matter much anyway. In spite of my conversations with Mr. Serizawa I was still planning to move away from Los Angeles. Maybe if they got their stuff together I'd move back. I wasn't sure. I certainly didn't expect them to ever get it together after what I'd seen. I'd be gone in a month. I just felt like I didn't want to leave it unsaid. When we parked out in front of her house I mustered up my courage and made my confession.

I expected at best she'd think it was sweet. She was far too beautiful to be interested in the likes of me, and at twenty-seven far too young. To my utter shock she told me she felt the same way about me.

"Don't try to kiss me," she said when I leaned in close. I wasn't. Or maybe I was. Who knows? But I didn't. We parted that night with no more than a friendly hug.

Within a week we were making out at a deserted lifeguard station on Manhattan Beach like a couple of horny teenagers.

I didn't tell Yuka everything. There was no reason to deliberately try to hurt her. But I told her enough. She knew that when I left the house in the evenings those weeks I was going to see Leilani. This made her comfortable enough at last to confess that she'd been seeing someone too. She said her being so cold to me for such a long time had a lot to do with that. So this had been going on for quite a while. I wasn't shocked. I wasn't even angry. Too much had gone down for that.

Yuka and I talked for a long time on several occasions and decided we needed to spend some time apart seeing where things led. But we still hadn't figured out what to do about our living situation. In just over a month my steady income would be gone, and we'd have to leave the apartment Nakano Productions had been paying for, for the past three years. Yet neither of us had a clue where to go.

Just then life intervened. I returned home one evening after hanging out with Leilani on the beach to find the toilet in the front bathroom full to the brim with murky brown water. I plunged it and everything seemed okay, so I went to bed.

The next morning I checked in on the bathroom and found the floor covered by nearly two inches of foul-smelling, brownish-green water that was literally flowing out of the toilet bowl like it was a really gross ornamental fountain. I saw bits of other people's toilet paper — I never use green toilet paper with flower prints — and undigested corn in there. *And* it was flowing out of the drains of both bathtubs as well. I tried calling the building superintendent, but he wasn't picking up his phone. So I ran upstairs to his apartment and found his girlfriend, who said she'd go wake him up. It took another half hour for him to make it down the two stories to my place. By that time the gooey water had risen another inch and was seeping into the carpet in the adjoining room. I threw some newspapers into the muck to try and absorb some of it, but to little avail.

Eventually he came and shut off the water then did a thoroughly half-assed job of cleaning up. Several hours later a couple plumbers showed up, in a very bad mood. They took one look at the mess and said, "This ain't a plumbing job. You gotta call a rooter guy!" Then one of the plumbers took me aside and said, "Look, buddy, I want to help you out. I really do. But the landlord here still owes us three grand for the last dozen plumbing jobs we did at this place. He never pays for anything. He's lucky we even came out here to check it out." They took a look at the superintendent frantically trying to get the water to go down the drain, shrugged, and trudged off, the muck on their shoes leaving ugly footprints on my carpet. Up till that day we had always taken our shoes off in the house!

The problem persisted for three more days. In spite of a half dozen calls to the superintendent's voice mail — he never picked up — no one came. I called the health department. The inspector who showed up said this was a definite violation and told me not to even set foot in the front bathroom. "There's germs all over that room," he said.

Luckily the rear bathroom still worked. But I didn't want to speculate on how long that would last. Now Yuka and I both had to start some serious house hunting.

Meanwhile, it just so happened that Jimmy, a guy I knew, was planning to leave his house in January. I asked if I might take over his place. The rent was about half what I was currently paying, and I just might be able to swing that if I could pull in a few freelance translation jobs or something. But Jimmy would be leaving on

January 15, and I needed to get out of my current place before I drowned in poop water.

I'd already arranged to spend Christmas at my sister's house in Knoxville. Getting my stuff into storage and then just going there without any intention of coming back to the apartment of shit would buy me a bit of time. I'd fly to my dad's place in Dallas, then make the drive from Dallas to Knoxville with him in the same van we'd driven up to Cincinnati with my mom in. He said it could be done in a single, very long day. I said okay as long as he agreed to do most of the driving.

But I had to make some kind of arrangements for where to stay once I returned. That's when I remembered that back in the summer, Greg Fain from the San Francisco Zen Center had invited me to spend New Year's Day at Tassajara as one of the people who looked after the place during the week between Christmas and New Years when there were no students or paying guests. I got hold of him to see if the offer still stood. It did. He had to be there anyway, and he was glad to have me come along. I shyly inquired if Leilani could be my guest, letting him know that all this was known by Yuka. Greg said that was fine.

The trip with Dad down to Knoxville was a far cry from the Zen Death Trip. There was no intermittent howling and no searching for handicapped toilets in the middle of the desert. Still, I missed having Mom there. It was our first Christmas without her, and the first one in a long time without Yuka. Still, with Stacey's two kids and their dogs and cats, it was hardly a lonely holiday.

I got through that okay and made it back to Los Angeles, where I spent a couple of nights at Yuka's new place while she was away at some out-of-town meeting for her job. Right after zazen class on December 29, I set off for Tassajara with Leilani.

# CHAPTER 36

# DOC MARTENS OUTSIDE THE DOOR

*I*t was a little weird setting off from the Saturday zazen class for Tassajara with Leilani. Most of the people who came to the zazen sittings at Hill Street Center didn't know about the troubles Yuka and I had been having the past year. My marital strife is not something I'm inclined to mention in a dharma talk or even in the conversations over lunch.

We got through it all right. If people wondered what was going on, they were too polite to say. It was a lovely drive up the coast on a gorgeous winter day. Or whatever passes for winter in California. When I lived in Ohio it took a long time for me to finally stop hating snow and cold. Now I miss it. But I enjoy the sunshine as much as anyone.

The drive into Tassajara from what they call the "gateway house," Greg told me, will destroy any normal car. So he arranged for us to get a ride with some folks who'd be driving in from the little residence they maintain in the nearest human settlement — you can't really call it a town — a place called Jamesburg.

Greg was right. Even driving the road to the gateway house was an event. Once you leave the highway the road gradually becomes narrower and the hills higher. At certain spots there are signs warning you to be careful not to run over the rare species of newt that inhabits the area. I wondered if you'd even be able to *see* a newt through the windshield of a moving car. After about an hour we came to the gateway house, where we were introduced to Steph and Lassa, who would drive us into Tassajara proper.

The drive up the dirt road to Tassajara sealed our retreat from civilization. I thought Hokyoji monastery in Minnesota was rural. But even their winding, mile-long driveway was nothing compared to the road to Tassajara. First you ascend to five thousand feet above sea level for about ten miles on a lumpy, bumpy one-lane dirt road, then you descend back down into the Carmel Valley for another four miles deep into the Ventana Wilderness Area of central California. If you can get through all fourteen miles in an hour, you're doing good.

Once in Tassajara you're almost completely cut off from the rest of humanity. There are no houses within miles of the place. There is a single telephone in the center, access to which is strictly limited. The stone cabin we'd be staying in had no electricity and could be heated only by a wood-burning stove. It did, however, have its own toilet with running water, making it one of the most luxurious accommodations in the center. In fact, the three stone cabins are so nice they don't let students stay in them during practice periods, lest too much jealousy arise toward those housed in them. But with no students or guests, the few of us there looking after the place got the coolest rooms. Spartan as it was, it was an extraordinary room indeed. I couldn't have asked for a better place to spend New Year's.

We were there over what they called the interim, a period between the end of the final practice period of 2007 and the beginning of the first practice period of 2008. Practice periods last three months, during which a rigorous schedule of zazen and work periods is observed, beginning with the wake-up bell at 3:30 a.m., and continuing until lights-out around 9 p.m. First-time students have it even worse. These students sit what's called *tangaryo*. For their first five days at Tassajara they are required to do zazen practice from 4:50 a.m. until 9 p.m. Even meals are taken while doing zazen. Toilet breaks are allowed, but other than that you just sit and sit and sit. Plus, you're not allowed to bathe while you're on *tangaryo* practice. Crazy stuff.

*Tangaryo* is a throwback to the old days when a typical prospective Zen student had to prove his true intention to follow the communal practice by waiting outside the temple for days or even weeks until someone finally took pity on the poor sod and opened the door. These days a lot of Zen centers practice some variation of *tangaryo*, though a lot of them don't bother. I've never done it and don't intend to. I'm not sure it's truly necessary.

I'll admit, though, it *is* a very good way to weed out the slackers. When you're running an isolated practice-center like Tassajara you cannot deal with anyone who isn't totally committed. A little tough practice at the outset can keep the place from being overrun by lazy bums who won't pull their weight. Considering all the bitching and moaning I have to listen to at our incredibly gentle and easy retreats (see chapter 28!) I can see where *tangaryo* could be very effective.

In any case, Leilani and I were not required to do *tangaryo*. In fact, we weren't required to do zazen at all. But we sat at the zendo every morning and night while we were there anyway. What surprised me about that was that we always sat alone except for the night of New Year's Eve, when the residents had a special zazen practice from 6 to 9 p.m.

This lack of anyone else doing zazen during break period kind of bummed me out. They say a glass of wine a day is a good thing for your circulation and cholesterol levels. That's seven glasses a week. But drinking all seven glasses on Saturday night is not the same thing. Intensive retreats and *sesshins* from time to time are very good. I'd recommend that any serious Zen student do at least one *sesshin* or retreat of at least two or three days every year. But the most vital zazen practice is the practice you do every day. There should be no breaks or vacations in zazen practice. It should be like brushing your teeth or showering, something you wouldn't even consider going without for a day, whether or not someone was there cracking the whip and forcing you to do it.

With no meditation practice required, the fifteen or so people who were there for the interim were mostly just supposed to help keep the place from falling into total disrepair during the period between the practice intensives. We all put in a few hours of work each day on some easy projects and were free to lounge around in the hot springs or hike or read books or whatever the rest of the time.

A few years back a book came out called *Shoes Outside the Door*, all about the sex scandals that rocked Tassajara in the early eighties. Whenever their abbot Richard Baker had one of his conquests over to his cabin — perhaps the very stone cabin Leilani and I were sharing — her shoes sitting outside the door would serve as a giveaway. When I saw Leilani's Doc Martens sitting outside our cabin door each night I had to chuckle.

Leilani and I fucked way more than Richard Baker ever did, I'm sure. We'd been saving it up for weeks, having no place we could be alone. I had no idea sex could be that intense. As Zen Master Ikkyu said of his blind prostitute lover in the fourteenth century, her gentle touch turned my jade stalk into a pile driver. Or something like that, anyway.

Here I was, though, just like Richard Baker, just like the guy from Clouds in Water in Minneapolis, just like Chögyam Trungpa and Buddha only knows how many others, getting it on with one of

my students right there in the monastery. I'll bet you dollars to
donuts spiritual* teachers have been boning their students in monasteries ever since the first one was built.

The bad reasons that teachers screw their students have gotten
a mountain of press in recent years. There really *are* spiritual teachers who use their position to exploit young hotties who come looking for enlightenment, promising them untold celestial rewards for
a material roll in the hay. Moreover, most of us in this spiritual
teacher game are deeply nerdy people. Lots of us could never score
with the opposite sex (or the same sex, for those who prefer that)
until we reached a position of authority, thereby becoming suddenly
attractive, even though we spent most of our lives being ignored or
laughed at. A starving man or woman will tend to gorge him- or herself if suddenly faced with a smorgasbord. The same thing happens
to rock stars, actors, and artists, but they usually get away with it.

But there are also some good reasons spiritual teachers seem to
end up in the sack with their students so often. Those of us who teach
this so-called spiritual stuff are deeply interested in it. Lots of us have
invested our whole lives in it. It's really hard to find someone else
who shares that kind of real passion for self-exploration, and when
you meet someone who does it's almost always a student. The
romantic bonds that develop in these cases between teachers and students are often every bit as deep and true as those shared in any other
relationship. I'd even be so bold as to say that they can very well be
a whole lot deeper and truer than most.

The idea that the student is forever and always the powerless
victim in these relationships is ridiculous. The notion that such a relationship forever and always represents the betrayal of all the other
students of that teacher is born solely out of jealousy and spite and

---

* I know I've said that Buddhism isn't "spirituality." But, again, for the sake of this
  discussion I'm going to classify it as spiritual so that we all know we're talking about
  a unique kind of teacher/student relationship.

therefore not even worthy of discussion.* As Eastern forms of spirituality continue to gain popularity in the West, it is essential that we give up the notion of teachers as gods and learn to regard them as ordinary people with ordinary needs for companionship and love. Often in the case of the good relationships that develop under these conditions, the student is one of the few people, if not the only person, the teacher regularly interacts with who allows him or her to be a human being, who doesn't expect the illusion of 24/7 saintliness. As I've become more famous in this game, meeting people who don't regard me as something otherworldly has become a much more valuable thing. Having a strong relationship like this, even if it's with a student, can allow the teacher to be more real with everyone he or she comes into contact with. Far from being a disgusting aberration, such relationships can make the real truth of human life clearer for everyone involved.

I learned a lot about Leilani on that trip. She was something special. There was a connection between us that went beyond anything I'd felt before. What we shared went far deeper than what mere coincidence could account for. But then again, I've never believed we encounter people at random. Still, she was, at least by most people's reckoning, my student. What did that mean for her in terms of the relationship and the bond that was now clearly forming between us?

As to whether a student should, or even can, remain a student in this kind of a relationship, my answer is a most definitive and unqualified *I have no idea.* On the one hand, nobody would ever say that a math teacher shouldn't help her boyfriend with his algebra. In making matters related to spirituality somehow apart from such things we're still stuck in the mode of regarding the teacher as something more than human. On the other hand, trying to continue the

---

* By the way, are you noticing the qualifiers "forever and always?" Good. Because sometimes teacher/student romances definitely *are* matters of powerless victims and *do* represent the betrayal of other students. Just not forever and always, okay?

student/teacher relationship when a romance has developed between the two is a unique and difficult matter. I would say that it is not impossible for the teacher/student relationship to continue when a romance develops between them. But a romantically entwined teacher/student relationship cannot be like the more standard teacher/student relationship. The only factor that would make romantic relationships between spiritual teachers and their students impossible is when teacher and student cling to the absurd notion that the teacher is more powerful than the student or the equally ridiculous idea that learning flows in only one direction.

No decent Zen teacher would stop teaching Zen, no matter who they went out with. And if the person they're dating is interested in Zen, that teacher will always be more than happy to share her experiences and understanding with the person she loves.

I knew that embarking on a relationship with Leilani would open me up to charges of hypocrisy and misuse of sexuality. And, friends, believe me, we misused sex in about a thousand new and exciting ways that week! But we knew what we were doing better than anyone who might accuse us of whatever they wanted to accuse us of. That was enough.

# CHAPTER 37

# THE END(?)

$S$ometime during the night the fire in the wood stove cooled and died. Leilani and I lay under the covers entwined in each other's arms to battle the bitter cold creeping through the stone walls. I saw the side of her sleeping face in the first rays of the New Year's dawn. She looked so pretty, I could almost forget the long chain of heartbreak that had brought us together.

2007 was a hell of a year for me. But I made it through. 2008 began on a far more agreeable note. But nothing is ever one way or another.

I recently attended a guided meditation session just to see what it was like. As I've said, zazen, unlike guided meditation, is completely undirected. You just sit there and whatever comes up, comes up. In guided meditation an experienced meditator talks you through the process and tries to lead you to whatever state of mind he or she thinks would be best for you. At one point in this particular meditation session, the leader said, "What are you thinking of right now? Is it pleasant or unpleasant?" We were supposed to label our thoughts

as one or the other. At that particular moment I happened to be thinking of Leilani. It was a few months after the events described in this
book, and a lot had happened between us. She was back up in Tassajara on a work practice period that was supposed to last six months,
while I was in Santa Monica feeling lonely. I'll save the rest of that
story for my next book! Anyway, I found that I couldn't possibly
label my thoughts as pleasant *or* unpleasant. And not just my
thoughts about Leilani. I couldn't fit any of the things I thought or
experienced into either of those boxes. I'm not sure if that was the
point of the exercise or not. But I don't think it was, because the
leader went off in a completely different direction with it, which disappointed me. Oh, well.

In any case, I think that by most people's way of reckoning
things, or indeed my own way of reckoning things before I started
doing all this Zen stuff, any year in which you lose your mom and
your grandma and your wife and your job would have to be characterized as a pretty unpleasant year. But I don't feel that way about it.
Heaven is just the other face of hell, and hell is just the other face of
heaven. They're two sides of the same coin. Neither can exist without the other.

As I write this, 2008 is already halfway over. By the time you
read this it'll be done. Was your year pleasant or unpleasant? So far
mine's been plenty of both.

The new management of Nakano Productions is far more sensible than the old one. They asked me to return to the fold and be
their creative liaison for the American-made Zone Robo movie project they intend to launch. So I'm still in Los Angeles. I've been to
Tassajara a few more times. Right now the place is surrounded by
fires, and all but the most essential personnel have been evacuated. I
hope they make it. By the time you read this you'll know if they did
or not, but as I write these words nobody's quite certain if the place
will be there by year's end or not.

I'm continuing my work as a Zen teacher and a writer, continually trying to find new ways to express what I've learned from my practice. Over and over and over again I fail. I've become popular enough that I'm now getting calls from journalists trying to get the "Buddhist angle" on this or that story. I talk to them for half an hour, and they distill what I've said down to three or four words that they get completely wrong. Those sound bites live on, and months later someone gets up in my face and demands to know how I could have said such a thing. So it goes.

This book stands as yet another failed attempt to convey what no one has ever succeeded in conveying. I'm sure people will have all kinds of detailed opinions about what I've said here. People I don't know from a package of Hostess Ding Dongs will write in to tell me all the things I should have done, all the things I should have said. Maybe in some sense there were things I could have handled differently, better. But "could have" is an illusion, and illusions are mostly useless. This is what I did. And only what I did really matters. I'm also certain that Gummo and Zeppo will weigh in with their versions of what *really* happened with them. Just like in that movie *Rashomon*, their versions will differ significantly from mine. But the only deliberate distortions I've made in this book were ones intended to protect those who need protection. What I've revealed here needed to be revealed, and there was no way to do it other than the way I've done it.*

Of course, what I've been trying to convey here isn't just about Zeppo and Gummo** or about spiritual organizations. It's about what really goes on in the life of a Zen teacher. That doesn't mean all of

---

\* I said what I said about them because people need to be aware of what actually goes on in spiritual organizations and, for once, they need to hear it from an actual current member of the organization in question rather than from a third party or from a disgruntled former cult follower. If you still want to believe in the existence of organizations so spiritually pure that things like what I've described in these pages never happen, I won't try and stop you. But I don't believe in such things.

\*\* I fully expect both of them, especially Gummo, to assume it is, though!

us are running around smoking dope* and doing our students. My life is unique to me. But we all have real lives beneath the robes and the dharma talks. Those real lives are what we draw on to make our practice what it is. My life is certainly not exemplary. But, really, nobody's is if you compare it to your own illusions of perfection. This much I guarantee you.

I originally picked the title of this book, *Zen Wrapped in Karma Dipped in Chocolate*, just because it sounded funny. It was nothing more than a label to put on the group of files in my computer that constituted the beginnings of a book. It comes from a yogurt commercial in which two new agey women are trying to find the proper adjectives to describe some delicious new flavor.

Surprisingly, the title turned out to be a pretty fair description of how this year has been for me. My Zen was wrapped up in plenty of my own karma — the fruits of my past actions. As for it being dipped in chocolate, even with all the big changes, things have been working out pretty nicely. The practice has allowed me to weather all that stuff in ways I never could have before I'd begun. It hasn't always been easy. But even when it hasn't been easy it's been less difficult than it would have been without the practice. And I've learned things from my suffering that I could not have learned in any other way.

As for enlightenment, that's just for people who can't face reality.

---

* And hating it. Please don't miss that part.

# ABOUT THE AUTHOR

**B**rad Warner was born in 1964 in Hamilton, Ohio and lived in a suburb of Akron until he was eight years old when his father took a job with the Firestone Tire Company's new plant in Nairobi, Kenya. Brad returned from Africa to the Akron area three years later with a different perspective on the world. In 1982 he joined the hardcore punk band Zero Defex (oDFx) whose song "Drop the A-Bomb On Me!" can be found on the P.E.A.C.E./War compilation. Around this time he began studying Zen with Tim McCarthy of the Kent Zendo. In the eighties he released five albums of neo-psychedelic rock on the Midnight Records label under the name Dimentia 13. In 1993 he moved to Japan and the following year fulfilled a childhood dream by getting a job working for a company that made cheesy giant monster movies. That same year he met Gudo Wafu Nishijima, an iconoclastic Zen teacher who published the only complete English translation of Dogen's masterwork, *Shobogenzo*. Brad was ordained a Buddhist monk by Nishijima in the late nineties. In 2004 he returned to America and now lives in Los Angeles. His websites are http://homepage.mac.com/doubtboy and http://hardcorezen.blogspot.com. He also writes a column for the Suicide Girls website: www.suicidegirls.com.